SACRED MAGIC

A Path for the Reintegration of the Human Being

This edition is a translation of *Sacred Magic: A Path for the Reintegration of the Human Being* by Massimo Scaligero, originally published in 1966 as *Magia Sacra. Una via per la reintegrazione dell'uomo* by Tilopa in Rome.

All rights reserved. No part of this book may be reproduced or transmitted in any manner, without prior permission by the publisher, except for purposes of research, review, criticism, or private study.

Published with the support of the Fern Hill Fund

ISBN: 979-8-9911570-0-1

First English edition

Translation copyright 2026 © Eric L. Bisbocci

Publication made possible through the collaboration with
Associazione Culturale Fondazione Massimo Scaligero
Published in 2026
By Alkion Press
330 Route 21, Ghent, NY 12075

Title: *Sacred Magic: A Path for the Reintegration of the Human Being*

Author: Massimo Scaligero
Translation: Eric L. Bisbocci
Layout and Design: Ella Manor Lapointe.
Cover Art: Martina Angela Müller

Massimo Scaligero

SACRED MAGIC

A Path for the Reintegration of the Human Being

Translated by
Eric L. Bisbocci

This translation is dedicated to Wilhelm (Willi) Müller and Ilse Kolbuszowski, who upon my re-entry to Eugene, Oregon from Italy in 1981 welcomed me to the Anthroposophical study group they helped found and guided me to a greater understanding of what lay before me...

Be awake. Since the Light was restored there is no earthly mineral that does not have its flash of lightning. This is the secret of the "ancient stone".

—*Raimondo Lullo*

Contents

1. The Cerebral Human Being 9
2. Self-Consciousness and Tradition 21
3. On Magical Perception 41
4. The Essence of Meditating 53
5. The Liberated Mental Sphere 73
6. Spirit and Rhetoric 97
7. The Science of Perennial Thinking 113
8. The Archetypes (*). Stellar Perception 133
9. Magical Consciousness 151
10. Operatio Solis 169

1.

THE CEREBRAL HUMAN BEING

Notwithstanding the era that presumes to have the ultimate understanding, the ultimate logic, and the ultimate positivism, we are still unaware today that, ordinarily, the world is thought devoid of thinking. Therefore, nothing of what we think is (itself) thought.

True thinking that thinks the world, operates unknown, unrecognized as the force by means of which we perceive the world, which is not the world already thought, or knowledge, or the being that we take pleasure in philosophizing about but, rather, the being for which we are alive.

Thought cannot be returned to things, as long as we ignore thinking them devoid of the thought that is their foundation. For this reason, they are had as alterity, which is *itself* real by virtue of the thinking that is unaware of itself and that knows only the extinguishing of its own movement. Devoid of inner life, the world emerges objectively as "matter." It is almost as if it has the foundation within itself and not in that which, as a foundation, is merely thought.

Therefore, matter is the 'perceived' that we are unaware of thinking and that is continually removed from its being, as well as from its thinking. Thus removed, or abstracted, it becomes the substance by means of which the edifice of culture is constructed—the impenetrable alterity, consecrated by an investigation devoid of the investigator; because in truth it is devoid of thought.

The alterity is the mere reflection of thinking, thought of as real apart from thinking. It is the projection of a world whose reality is avoided, because it is unconsciously feared, owing to a thinking that is unperceived, since in rationality the life that lies at its foundation is eliminated, namely the life by means of which we feel and will, outside its relation to thought.

Therefore, today's spiritual practitioners, experiencing thought, tend to encounter, in their inner depths, the underlying forces of feeling and of willing, conjoined with the world. Because the world really is not devoid of thought, except for those who ignore how in perceiving they already encounter the thinking of the world without needing to think it. They encounter it, however, in the areas in which they sleep and dream.

In binding to cerebralism, the profound forces of feeling and willing that encounter the world estrange themselves from their original nature—so that, in thinking, we lose the world's substantiality.

True thinking that thinks the world, operates unknown. The work of the spiritual practitioner is, therefore, to become independent of the head system.

***

In overcoming abstractness, in rediscovering the virtue of the image of thought, researchers tend to become free of feeling and of willing, which, as forces having fallen into corporeality, acquire instinctive power through the central nervous system.

To be the "I" that we each feel we are, we work to disenchant its identification with the physical body. We turn to the experience of the incorporeal body, through a thinking free of abstractness, because in such thinking we can grasp the corporeal limits and the limitless being of the forces that edify it—namely, the forces in which we ordinarily think, without them being what we think. What we think in fact is its negation, just like the "dreamed" that is remembered or narrated is the negation of the dream's substance.

For us, to be independent of the dynamisms of the cerebral system is to be outside a corporeality unthinkable as a physical entity, and yet ordinarily thought of as such; to encounter the forces that govern corporeality according to a power alien to the head system.

In truth, an isolated corporeality in itself, with its own life processes, does not exist, just as the isolation of the head system from the rest of corporeality does not exist, except for a degree of consciousness that is drawn from the element that governs such a system—minerality.

***

Thanks to the structure of the nerve substance, our system of head forces is conditioned by earthly currents that govern the aspect of the manifestation that arises as minerality.

Subjected to the spirit in the blood, these currents can instead take hold of consciousness through the nerve substance, thereby conditioning the relationship between us and the world, and the value of this relationship to the life of the soul.

Dominators of that which as "matter" is lifeless, they make the inanimate and the lifeless within the mental (sphere)* count, by manipulating its light of life, of which the mental itself lives. Therefore, they are the spirits of falsehood.

It is the reason for which, by undergoing the vital influence of cerebralism, we are led to continue our own being and therefore our own existence, according to impulses of a nature that is no longer our own, but we functionally assume, as one of the vehicles of our presence in the world. Thus, through earthly experience, animality can arise in us as an instinctive current that compels us even in the mental (sphere), ascending into the vital forces that nourish the head, and manifesting, there, where these forces cease to be governed by the spirit. This is inevitable to us as modern human beings, but—as will be seen in the following considerations—not because our corporeal being is of an animal origin.

Conscious thought continuously opposes these vital forces. In order to be, it is destructive. Thought makes its way, there, where it eliminates such forces. But the elimination is never brought to completion. It does not give rise to a corresponding re-edification, as we—satisfied with the thinking by means of which we oppose nature—ignore it. We still lack the strength to perceive the movement through which we oppose such forces,

---

*   Mental (mentale) – This adjectival term is often meant by Scaligero to function as a noun. It refers to the sphere of mental activity connected to the mind, usually in relation to sense-based thought. I have occasionally coupled the term "mental" with "sphere" to remind the reader that is not simply a reference to the mind or brain per se.

the movement by means of which, if possessed, we would recreate nature.

Therefore, through the possibility of thinking the human ego reaffirms itself, creates for itself an egoic nature, which, on the one hand, intellectually opposes nature and, on the other, unconsciously reaffirms its dominance. It is the contradiction whereby human beings of the head are unknowingly inclined to express animality, while profound supra-sensory currents work to transform this animality through elevated forms of reason.

Thus, the highest thinking arises as the spirit's struggle against the nature that tends to become thought.

This struggle, not understood, not willingly assumed, appears to us in obscure forms of pain.

Willingly assumed, it is the knowledge that liberates us in nature, reveals the meaning of pain and, by ceasing to be a struggle, becomes the germ of brotherhood.

The highest thinking penetrates us precisely as that which is so absolute that it does not seem to be able to be had as thought. It is nevertheless thinking that unites the "I" with the reality of the world, by virtue of a communion, whose objectivity is its activity beyond cerebralism, which is to say, beyond the ego, beyond the common being, beyond the fear opposed to what—as the threshold of knowledge—is the sacrifice and annihilation of itself.

The bond to cerebralism is essentially the source of fear, because it interrupts the flow of the original forces within the soul. Such forces are obliged to enter the human being through obscure and unpredictable paths.

***

Regarding the physical or the metaphysical world, human culture today is typically a product of cerebralism. Constitutionally modern rationalists, regardless of their vocation, are cerebral people, for the fact that they are not yet truly thinking individuals. In them, thinking does not have the same objective force of its own organ as seeing has, for example, with respect to the eye.

But "cerebralism" as a system in itself does not exist. It can only exist as a vehicle of something else.

On the strictly physiological plane, the existence of the cerebral organ depends on the remaining corporeality. Therefore, instinctive life expresses itself functionally by means of this organ as a motion that rises from corporeality into the psyche, to which a limitation could be placed by an inverse motion, which penetrates into the psyche from non-corporeality. In that sense, the movement of thinking that uses its own organ can really be understood. But normal thought lacks such autonomy. The physical organ, which it should use, prevails over it, because it is not fully used; it is not mastered; it is not known.

The lack of autonomy with respect to its own organ explains the abstractness of thought. In essence, one feeds the other.

Abstractness hardly knows how to recognize itself, since any recognition of the kind is not able to escape from itself, from its own abstract limit, from dialectics—which, therefore, can be seen as a sign of thought's unfulfilled reality.

Therefore, in knowing, we modern humans mistake the perception of the inorganic world for a perception of the organic world, of which we are truly devoid.

Because we implement as thought, not the flow of the spirit via the nervous system—which is unknown to us—but what, as representation and concept, is reflected by such a system, we do not rise from the category of minerality. We are bound to the inorganic level. We do not escape from the lifeless aspect of the world. We only see physical phenomena. We only perceive the inorganic aspect of the organic. We imagine but do not perceive "the living." We assume it. We have it as thought, but we do not realize that we have it only as thought. We deceive ourselves of being able to act upon "the living," which for us—though manifesting itself to us—remains a mystery.

Looking at other beings, we truly do not see them, because we see only their minerality. What for us is truly invisible in the current earthly scene, is effectively ourselves; it is the human being. *There is no human being who sees another.* Therefore, brotherhood cannot exist.

***

That of the earth which is dead emerges as real.

The earth's living being is really invisible. Visible is only that of it which is bare mineral, elaborated by forces imperceptible to the senses. For those of us who really think, the form of things is idea. Visible is that which for the spirit exists as nonexistent, because it is always transcended in being perceived—the being which demands from it an unusual movement. This movement is the freedom actualized in the non-being that appears to be the being of minerality.

To see only what is dead is not the experience of reality, but the *temporary* experience of thought. By binding itself to the senses, thought gives body to that which is empty. It fills with "matter" the living being that it does not know how to perceive. It lacks the power to conceive an immaterial living being, a matter that leans on something other than itself and, yet, as matter it proves to be the unthinkable that one thinks, nor to remember that, in any case, even perceiving is quality. (For example, one thing is weight, another is measurement. But even measurement is an act of thinking.)

The only possibility of our relationship with such matter is not material. It is the mental picturing that represents everything to itself, but is still unable to know anything about itself.

The forms and colors of the world are that within which "matter" arises so as to disappear.

The world that we believe we know is not real. Assumed as real, it continuously falls apart. The continuous arrangement of the collapsed, as a mechanical art, gives the illusion that it has not collapsed and that it can, as a multiplicity, have its own organization of culture and of science.

That of the earth which is living does not belong to the earth. It arrives from other worlds. It enables the earth to partake in a non-terrestrial universe, where the rhythm that dominates in the earth through catastrophes, always re-orders chaotic matter, which in turn cannot be governed by any mechanical order.

That of the earth which is living is perceived by what lives in us. But we do not possess what lives in us and lives in the world. We perceive it within the guise that is its negation.

There are no modern rationalists who perceive the formative force of a plant and who, therefore, know that they cannot speak objectively about the forces of life, unless they perceive that they are only faced with justified assumptions.

The living being appears on earth, but not the visible earth. It is the invisible earth, which still cannot be grasped by the human being.

The living being can be newly perceived on earth, if we arouse it within our own interiority. It restores life to the thinking that, devoid of life, inevitably represents the earth devoid of life.

***

The present culture, being a cerebral product, is at a dead end, which it not only fails to overcome, but which it does not even recognize. It can perceive it on the condition of not knowing what it means.

Modern science is based on the fact that the intellect can only grasp of nature what is dead or perishes—not the "living." It does not suspect that it is building knowledge on an element of death and of being itself a lifeless structure. What present-day investigators are able to perceive and know, is only the lifeless aspect of things, which they believe to be real. Meanwhile, it is the lifeless reflection of a relationship that they actualize but that eludes them, since it belongs to them in the unconscious depths.

What can be perceived through the senses is that of the being which no longer exists, the mark left behind, the symbolic imprint, which, at that level, by conditioning thought, arouses the idea of life, but not life. While animating nature and beings, life remains unknown to us, due to our incapacity to distinguish practically, more than conceptually, sensory perception from thinking.

The distinction between thought and perception is not a philosophical fact, but an inner achievement which, as things currently stand, is the only one that can lead us to the source of our own being—namely of the being whose problem and its insolubility (which provide so much material and pretext to inexhaustible cultural arguments) are otherwise inevitable.

In reality, life lives only as a power of image or idea of the person who perceives and thinks. Only this power of image can be experienced as identical to the force of life that the intellect assumes beyond the perceived—in that dynamic identity remaining nevertheless extraneous to ordinary consciousness. That power of image manifests as life but, ordinarily, we have only its abstract reflection. We fail to notice that, of what we perceive, the only life that we could experience is simply our capacity to imagine life, which we continuously lose in perceiving. But, naturally, we lose it insofar as it is there.

There is a dying part of the earth that is visible, and a part that awakens to new life that is invisible. The part that dies is what we perceive and intellectually represent and exalt. Yet, simultaneously, there emerges from us—as a new invisible life of the earth—the inner imagining, or our capacity to imagine life, stimulated by sensory perceiving but concluded in unconsciousness, from which it remarkably frees itself as creative imagining, when, through spiritual practice, or the purification of pain, it becomes independent of the earth's past (that is) active by means of sensory contents.

Today, we know of nature only what is dead, and we consider this to be nature. But in such knowing, by cutting out life, we also reject morality. We can be religious or mystical, but we lack the possibility of moral life, because we do not gather, as an objective truth, the inner element of the things that we experience every day in their outer phenomenology. We lose their spiritual reality. Therefore, despite our intentions, we are in a state of falsehood in relation to our own cultural experience and in contradiction with our own inner calling. But dialectics masks the contradictions and puts the conscience at peace.

Scientists, or rationalists, investigating nature by means of the intellect, really know nature by what is akin to its dying; but they ignore it, or behave as if they ignored it. It must be said that they are scientists of a certain empirical-systematic surface inclination, superficial aptitude, but for the rest of their being they are immersed in superstition. The magisterium of science nowadays does not suit those who call themselves scientists, except in very rare cases.

Knowing is dead, yet it gives itself an automatic life, whose only obvious production on the physical plane is the machine; on the inner plane it is a logical-intellectualistic systemization.

In effect, what we as realistic human beings lack today is precisely the experience that we presume to possess—namely, that of reality. We call something we possess only in abstract images and measurements, reality. Yet, it is obvious that we can have such an abstract relationship with things, thanks to a profound relationship, which escapes us as a conscious fact.

The art of realistic researchers should be to start from what they already realize about themselves in activities such as thinking and perceiving—from which they draw fundamental forms of certainty—and to verify not dialectically, but experientially, what manifests within them through such activities. If we can remain independent of gnoseological or psycho-physiological presuppositions regarding such an investigation, we arrive at recognizing the objective necessity of an inner experimentation, without which science nowadays no longer makes sense. And if it places itself along the line of such experimentation, we can begin to perceive a vital element deep within ourselves, which is simultaneously within the inner depths of things, as an objective event.

Our knowledge begins to count as reality, when we are able to recognize the character of lifelessness of what we know so far only by excluding this element of life, and place this in relation to the fact that what we ordinarily think and translate into thought is akin in its lifelessness to what in us is lifeless—the system of nerves; to whose mediation we owe the present form of perceiving and mental picturing.

Where we human beings are not inwardly alive, we are dominated by the life of nature.

***

It is necessary to distinguish the force of life that edifies terrestrial forms, from the force of life represented and imagined. The first could only be perception: only those who truly perceive it would be able to speak about it. Regarding the other, only those who have no interest in perceiving it, or in knowing it, but only in projecting it into a knowledge, can speak.

Knowledge is the negation of thought.

Training ourselves to make the idea of the life force rise before us, to provoke its image, is the path for it to become perception. This possibility emerges as the perception of thinking within sensory perceiving.

Sensory perception is only partially a physical process. Only the stimulus belongs to the sensory sphere, as well as the neuro-sensorial mediation, but the act of perceiving is always non-sensory. We can recognize it as supra-sensory, wherever its pure content becomes direct experience.

In every sensory perception the pure content is present, but unconscious.

The pure content is living, but we only become conscious of that of it which ceases to be alive, as ordinary sensory experience.

In the human being, the force of life operates according to the spirit, there, where it is not counteracted by the movements of consciousness. Nevertheless, in the functions of nature, such work is confined to processes outside its movement.

Future human culture will depend on our ability to perceive the "living," just as for now we merely perceive its reflection, that is, the lifeless resonance in the form of sensation and mental picturing. The 'living', as an incarnated spiritual force, is independent of nature only as a structural power, not as a life necessitated by fixed natural laws.

In this sense, we are constituted in such a way that what is vital in us retains the spirit in itself as a force of life; it does not allow it to flow. This is the contradiction that must be understood. The spirit can flow free only through that which, not embodying it as life, does not offer resistance.

Only where life is extinguished and eliminated does the spirit become conscious. By extinguishing life, the spirit finds the path to its own expression within the human being.

This dying has different forms in the degrees of being and in time. Pain, self-extinction and knowledge operate according to a pure, single inner movement.

In modern times, what manifests the life of the blood, as a mystical or heroic exaltation, is the spirit possessed by life, more than life possessed by the spirit. It is the ennoblement of ordinary human beings, not their transcendence.

In humans today, only what extinguishes life, through the inner processes of consciousness, can open the door to the spirit. Heroism and mystical abnegation tend to be radical experiences of the soul, more than events of the outer scene. They can express themselves, in fact, to the extent that they are inner acts. The fact and the act tend to coincide.

Thus, only thought, insofar as it dies, can produce the void in which the power of thought is the spirit that is about to find life again.

Pure death is possible only for life, insofar as it arises from the void of thought. But along the same lines, the purification of pain, being the dissolution of the egoic human being—bound to cerebralism—operates like profound thought.

There is no other way to overcome longing and to extinguish the processes by which it implies death as an extreme proof of nature's powerlessness to retain life.

In reality, the human body is righteous and permeated by supra-sensory forces, and it is so essentially structured by them, that it could not die. Our physical body is so structured that it should be immortal. But we cut off the currents of immortality. We continuously annihilate its work. We destroy the body to experience egoic consciousness, individual existence, the yearning for existence. In reality, we become sick and die, because for now we are only cerebral human beings.

Cerebralism is the source of fear. But we ignore this and believe we escape unconscious fear, by converting into culture, into scientific activity, into the persuasion of progress, into physical and metaphysical myths its connection to cerebralism. Meanwhile, our task would be to know it, so as to draw from it the secret of life, the art of freedom and of fraternity.

2.

Self-Consciousness and Tradition

The processes of nature, manifesting by means of the nervous system, subconsciously, are conductors of forces that tend to shape our iner life, so that we believe our longing and existence to be our own.

To those who know the course of the Tradition, it turns out how at one time such forces, in their cosmic movement, operated positively upon us, while aiming to affirm themselves through our consciousness. They provided nourishment for our inner life, on the condition of dominating it. This was possible because the spirit expressed itself in vital processes to surface as consciousness, as it was not yet self-consciousness.

Self-consciousness, in splitting off from the spiritual processes that nonetheless continue to edify its physical support, arises naturally insofar as it is opposes consciousness.

With the birth of self-consciousness, the orienting work of those cosmic forces—whose observance was the Tradition—begins to be a fact adverse to the human spirit, tending to take it back to past stages by repeating within us an ancient movement, which even then was not an original movement, but that which had the task of binding the original human being to the metaphysical and physical earth.

For a long phase of human development and culture, the work within us of those inner cosmic forces was necessary for us to become earthly.

Such forces cannot but feel adverse to the element of freedom where the spiritual principle of the human being re-surfaces. For this reason, they tend to distract us from ourselves through myths and dreamy states. They continue today to work in the human interiority, and they can dominate it intimately to the degree that they make use of reflected thinking, which does not have sufficient autonomy to notice this interiority. They operate through modern myths, or myths of the past, capable of soliciting soul forces, which elude the pure principle of the "I."

In this sense, we can intuit the meaning of Yoga and of traditional disciplines. They were the human art of nurturing the communion of consciousness with its metaphysical base and to give life meaning through this foundation. Yet, we must ask ourselves what, within us, constitutes this metaphysical foundation.

In reality, the metaphysical foundation and the physical human structure used to coincide. There was no opposition between the life of the soul and nature, since nature was not separated from the spiritual by consciousness. To raise consciousness, however, original forces did not operate but, rather, cosmic forces endowed with the power of leading the original human toward earthliness—namely, supra-sensory entities bound by the need to assert the materiality of the cosmos, both metaphysically and physically, and of giving spiritual consistency on earth not to the original human being, but to the fallen human being.

For fallen human beings, regularity meant conforming to the immediate spiritual, which replaced the original. The wisdom of their guides was an art of listening to the super-human and leading human beings to conform to it, through spiritual practice and rituals.

The repetition of this conformation, as a traditional fact, the tendency to realize again that regularity, is today irregular, since the relationship between consciousness and nature is inverted, given that we have awakened as self-conscious beings from the lower projection of nature, namely in that which is our death.

***

There is a moment in human history where the original spiritual entities ceased to operate in our interiority, as the conscious principle began to blossom within us. They continued their supportive work precisely in allowing our self-consciousness and our capacity for self-determination, to arise intact. Meanwhile, other entities that belong to an *intermediate* world continued operating in us according to the ancient movement, by tending to direct the action that now wanted to spring forth in us from the pure individual principle. In this way, they impeded the realization of our freedom, namely what would remove from us the possibility of feeding off the nascent forces of the soul.

In human souls, these entities operate by aiming to exclude the "I," not only through collective persuasions and myths of modern civilization, but by way of certain human areas suited to the spiritual, through mysticisms and metaphysics of the past, whose regularity was based on the fact that the original hierarchies operated in place of the "I." Spiritual practitioners then experienced the "I" outside of the earthly (realm). Their art was to encounter the "I" outside the sensory (realm). This "I" today is individualized in them, emerging as self-consciousness. The "I am," once encountered by rare initiates in the extra-terrestrial cosmos, today is on Earth. The One whom the Tradition awaited is present as the Spirit of the Earth.

It can be said that the current aim of yoga, of the pseudo-tradition and of a great part of Eastern and Western occult paths is to, unconsciously, hold us back in the world of instincts and to render us powerless before the culture of matter and the machine, through spiritualistic pretexts—behind which urge the action of the impersonal powers adverse to human beings, which particularly rely on our incapacity to recognize them.

***

The spirit governs the physical processes everywhere in the human organism, except in the system of head. Here, it would manifest its order, where it could express itself without any mediation, as thought. Instead, it can express itself as dialectical thought, to the extent that its force, being reflected in cerebralism, manifests in reverse.

We modern humans think in the inverted forces of the spirit. And by means of the inverse spirit, we presume to grasp the spiritual.

Through this functional inversion, in the thinking individual, it is inevitable today, that the highest qualities become—save rare exceptions—the opposite of what they are spiritually. Love becomes hatred, perfidy, cruelty; courage becomes cowardliness, generosity, stinginess and envy.

It is our present-day dilemma. By virtue of reflected consciousness, the spirit in us gets perverted without the possibility for us to know how this occurs, whereas at one time we received from traditional asceticism the means to evade instincts and passions. Such means were not an individual creation. They were donated to us, insofar as we observed certain ritualistic modalities. Today, such a relationship is no longer possible. Often powerless, researchers who, through spiritual practice, would come to open themselves up to the qualities of the spirit, would each time helplessly witness their deterioration and corruption.

There is no traditional asceticism that gives the researcher a way to notice how the reflectivity of thought is produced, since it is an experience unique to modern-day human beings.

The process of reflectivity occurs through the subconscious "inherence" of spiritual forces to the cerebral organ, in the sphere of a corporeality that they instead dominate in all the other organs and in the various processes of life. These are nearly always obstructed by the activity of consciousness, mediated by the central nervous system.

Thought devoid of life, as a reflection, compels feeling and the will to this deprivation—which therefore cannot but manifest corporeally, by resonating in the central nervous system. But at the corporeal level, they arise incompletely and as an alteration of what they truly are in their transcendence. They manifest as personal emotional-instinctive forces, deprived of height and vastness. There, where they adhere to corporeality, they are transformed into their opposite, namely into a degrading egoism, against whose oppressions we combat in vain.

Due to thinking's fall into reflectivity, we can no longer know true feeling, nor true willing. *True mysticism, or true magic are no longer possible*. The willing that can be strengthened within us today thanks to our fanciful ambitions of dialectics or of power, cannot but be the vehicle of an inferior magic.

Therefore, those of us who seek the Tradition, without knowing what we have become—insofar as we lack the Tradition—will not be able to find it again. We will be unable to be continuators of it.

Some take pleasure in speaking about the Tradition, and in writing with authority and philological preparation on it, precisely because they have no other way of making contact with it. But they do not even remotely suspect how their existence should radically change and their traditionalistic dialectics extinguish itself, if their lives were to be minimally invested by grandiose forces that act within the "Tradition." But there is no danger that this will happen, since their task is to disturb those who cultivate the correct meditation and to hinder the possibility of opening the passage once again to such forces.

In truth, the profound work that we insist on with regards to thought, is for the resurrection of the powers of feeling and willing—whose echo, no less, for the present-day cerebral and rational human being has died out—so that every foolish ambition to restore life to the Tradition, which eludes such work or presumes to do so by "traditional" means, is a latent opposition to it.

***

Thought, as a reflected activity of the spirit, while remaining in itself a supra-sensory movement, in its discursive expression, depends on the cerebral apparatus that reflects it.

Reflected thought lacks life, even though it has within itself the movement of being reflected. It is a movement that is *used, not possessed*, by thinking human beings, since it is a moment of the thinking determination—the one spoken of by idealism and which idealism has never really been able to grasp, because it has always been inevitable for it to view it speculatively, not as an inner experience possible beyond dialectics. It is instead an experience possible only beyond dialectics, that is, insofar as dialectical movement is possessed, just as perception is possessed.

The thinking that is thought is not identical to the movement by means of which one thinks. This movement is the true thinking; it is more important than thought. But it is not possessed. We are beings that think in order to be able one day to have this movement; but this is not known, because the whole of nature itself accustomed to using thought, refuses to be recognized by thought.

As ordinary humans, we are more interested in the object of thought than in thought, even when, philosophically, the object is thought, itself. We do not assume that the object is given to us by way of thought, not thought by way of the object. True thinking is already one with the object and operates within it, for the fact that it appears as an object. Objectivity is already a category of thought.

Still, thinking does not matter as much as the thoughts to which it gives rise. Insofar as we are bound to our own nature, each of us is bound to our "own" thoughts. Each of us cares about our "own" opinions. We make them objects of thought—objects to which we exclusively give importance by means of thought, and we establish values such as civilization, culture, sociality, spirit, tradition, ethics, and mysticism, but we cannot really will what we think, because we do not possess the life of thought by means of which we think.

This is our mental limitation as human beings, regardless of our vocation. For example, we will never know an ancient spiritual practice like Zen, for we do not possess the knowing by means of which we immediately grasp it and pose it to ourselves. Whereas, at one time, Zen did not pass to the disciple through discourse or doctrine, but primarily through the flash of creative imagination.

Freedom of thought consists exclusively in its being reflected and therefore in not being conditioned by its spiritual foundation. In being reflected, the spirit is present as consciousness endowed only with virtual life. Virtual consciousness, however, depends so much on the vital processes of the reflecting organ, which goes missing with the suspension of this organ—in sleep, in half-sleep, in fainting spells.

The support is removed from consciousness when it is so needed by the vital processes as to exclude any movement that is not that of the spirit as a virtue of life: life still being, for us, sleeping consciousness.

The freedom that we achieve in thought is devoid of reality, because it is abstract. It lacks the power of life, since life is the pre-reflected movement of thinking, which we, by thinking, do not implement but extinguish to be awake, and yet do not perceive. We sleep, with regard to this pre-reflected movement.

Meanwhile, we are awake only in the thinking seized by cerebralism; in the object of thought; in the contingent appearing of things, or in the abstract void.

***

The virtual freedom of thought is the spirit's presence in reflectivity, for which the spirit is able to will in the reflected order anything independently of nature and of the ironclad determination of the physical world, without, however, possessing such will.

The spirit is able to will itself in consciousness, but reflectively—namely, dialectically. Such willing remains abstract, devoid of a relationship with the reality perceived by means of the senses.

Any relation between abstract perceiving and the sensory world, is but outer and contingent. This relation, by having to limit itself to semblance and measurability, which assume the total role of reality, at most, gives rise to mechanical creation and rationalistic culture. Not grasping of reality except what is deprived of the unconscious mediation at work in perceiving, it flows into a knowledge and into a culture, where individuals will have to struggle vigorously to become free, if they wish to achieve a concrete relationship with the world.

But thought—as the Initiate of the new times* teaches—gives itself solely for its own ascesis. Abstract freedom, proper to thinking, can draw from the life of which it is reflected. The spirit can will itself in reflected thought and insist on this self-willing, until overcoming the limit of reflectivity. It can will itself in thought as a force of life capable of rendering its virtual freedom real. The life creating movement itself flows within the thinking that frees itself.

Freed thinking is the extinction of reflected thought. Therefore, *reflected thought is to be possessed*, because initially it is the only one that can truly be possessed by the "I."

Spiritual practitioners must extinguish the thinking that they think they possess, but do not. To extinguish it, they must possess it. To possess it, they must first experience it objectively in the sensory (realm); they must know it to the extent that it manifests through its sensory contents. *There is no other way*

---
*   Rudolf Steiner

to know it. Therefore, it can only be an experience of modern human beings. There is no tradition that offers the possibility of experiencing the "I" by means of objective thought.

To extinguish thought, the investigator must first of all remove it from sensory contents, from scientific and mathematical form, or logic, by means of which it has become objectified. Therefore, logic, mathematics and science have been and still are necessary..

This means that investigators can experience it as pure form, only to the extent that this form has been able to take on the sensory world. They free it from the identity with this world, managing, by way of the thinking ascesis, to have as a content, the formal power itself by means of which they think. It is a formal power that directly manifests within sensory perceiving, but unconscious. The content of perceiving, in fact, as we will see, is always internal. Only the stimulus is physical. The meaning of all modern human experience lies in the possibility to volitionally experience such an immaterial content.

By experiencing the inner power of perceiving and retracing the extroverted dialecticism, through which daily the physical and metaphysical being is represented, the investigator can enter the creative current of thinking, which will reveal itself as more-than-thinking, namely as the very power that enlivens nature and moves worlds.

To extinguish thought, investigators must possess it. To possess it, they must know the art of concentration, which cannot be taught by whoever has not received it from the spiritual world itself. It is the art that can even be taught in human terms, but on condition of having been known as a superhuman gift by the person who intends to teach it.

To extinguish thought is to rediscover the thinking that thinks independently of the head support, namely the thinking from which springs the ordinary possibility of thought and of consciousness.

***

Within the functions of nature, the spirit manifests as the processing power of the earthly element, but opposed to the conscious human being.

To manifest as corporeality, our spirit must operate in concert with the forces of the earth and of the cosmos, by achieving a physical form, which lives on the condition of opposing it, there, where it continues its work as an incorporeal individual entity. For this reason, such form can be the support to consciousness.

The "manifesting" of the spirit cannot be grasped in its relation to the corporeal functions and processes, because in these the spirit renounces its own original motion, to adapt to earthly laws. The spirit can instead be intuited in the architecture that is purely physical, in the structural element of corporeality, but not because we concentrate on the sensory form of the bodily organs, which would lead into obtuse, sub-sensory areas.

We cannot arrive at perceiving the spirit in that structural element by means of an inner activity bound to the natural functions, but only by freeing this (activity) from their need and re-ascending to the supra-sensory structure of the organs, which is the work of free thought.

***

We cannot approach anything except through thinking. There is no vital process, or current of force that can be aroused by us, which does not come to meet us insofar as we are already the ones to encounter it by means of immediate thought. Thought operates without having opposition before it that is not thought, itself. There is no matter or thing opposed to thought, which is not matter or a thing already interpenetrated with thought.

We perceive, but a part of our perceiving is already thought, itself. Naturally, it has nothing to do with rational thinking, but with immediate "springing" thought that can be experienced as such—namely, as pure thinking, or thinking in its free state, within the inner structure of perception.

Sensations always arise with respect to a consciousness. This is an observation that does not mean an idealistic thwarting of reality but, rather, an identification of the point at which the ideal and the real coincide objectively, yet unconsciously. In every knowing, this coincidence is already taking place, even if we are unaware of it. The task of thought is to notice what it already accomplishes.

Thought is experienced as the profound mediator, above as below, regardless of the object, given that it is always its internal form.

Wherever thinking penetrates, the processes of nature become extinct.

Beyond the processes of nature extinct in the human person, the spirit operates as an individual virtue of life. Then it can extinguish thought, by way of its deeper motion of life.

The extinction already begins with the juxtaposition from which consciousness arises on the basis of an unconscious process, but continues in the movement typical of thought. It can draw from its own inextinguishable being, where it becomes increasingly conscious, until becoming a volitional possibility and, in that sense, autonomous, namely consciousness grasping itself on this side of what is its immediate support, and yet, on this side of what it needs to extinguish.

The extinction is the vehicle by means of which the spiritual being opens a passage in the soul, annihilating its identification with nature—thereby beginning the formation of a new nature.

To extinguish the processes of nature is not to impede longing, to renounce nourishing oneself, or to cease breathing, and so on, but rather, the independence of the inner activity from such processes and the subsequent possibility of penetrating its movement, by perceiving its own identity with it, ordinarily unaware.

The movement, unconverted, is longing.

Longing is not outside us. In the animal world, what appears as longing does not engage the spirit; it is not longing.

Those who in silence know how to contemplate moments of life of the animal, of water or of the earth or of the air, can gather within themselves a profound substance that tends to rise again from animality, as original life. The animal's spontaneity is a sign that cannot be allowed to act within the soul, except by those who know, as their own thought, the thought that moves the dream of the animal world. It is the redemption of longing.

***

We encounter what is living of nature through the volitional forces that we do not notice and therefore do not control. We use them in the activity of the senses and in the movement of the limbs, having them only as a product. We do not know them as a productive virtue. We do not know we use them. In order to know them, we should distinguish the perceived from perceiving and perceiving from thinking. We should experience perception in the pure state, so as to encounter the original thinking within it.

We could indeed operate on the force of life, if we possessed the will with which we encounter it in sensory perceiving. But we are unaware that this will begins to possess us in logical thinking: yet always annihilating us in form and speech.

We humans say we will something, and this may be true. Yet, we do not possess this willing. We do not know where it comes from. We do not know how, from us, it manifests in objects.

We can experience this will as an immediate force, only if we bring to it the presence of the "I" just as we bring it—by willing—into conscious thought: in such conscious thinking we are already activating the immediate will.

The will encounters the world in ordinary perceiving, in an "area" where it cannot be conscious. The art of the spiritual practitioner is to perceive this area just as we perceive the sensory (realm) where willing takes place. Likewise, the will encounters the world within the movement of thought, but in that living moment which thought carries out but does not possess, since, there, where it is able to know it exists, it is already reflected, having become external to itself.

We can grasp this will within perceiving, if, by following the correct spiritual practice, we train ourselves to feel the architectural and synthetic power of perception, as an objective fact, and in this (perception) we concentrate, to the point of perceiving the intensity of the will for which the object arises before us as an image. According to this spiritual practice, we, as disciples, do not start with mythical esoteric representations, but with what we directly experience within ourselves.

If we grasp within ourselves the will that, foreign to consciousness, already by its own virtue meets the will of the world, in perception, we experience not that of nature which is dead, but that which is emerging, arising from the necessity of death, to become the secret of the earth.

Our presence—namely our perceiving, our imagining—as humans on earth is not indifferent to nature and to the world. Nature and the world are such because they become human experience, surfacing in an ulterior state of life.

Whether the earth subsists as a sidereal body beyond its processes of death, depends on our ability to overcome within ourselves the need to depend on such processes for knowledge and to consider fundamental a culture that in its lifeless state is provisional—deriving it from the provisional relationship that we establish with the world through cerebralism.

Being bound to what is dead in the process of knowing and, therefore, of culture, makes us free only in the dead part of our being, namely in that which is our abstract production. This prevents us from making our freedom a reality.

In fact, today, we give freedom only to what is dead within us, not to what is alive within us, since we are not conscious of what is alive within us. We know neither perceiving nor thinking, but only the perceived and the already-thought, and to these we are bound.

If we observe, we can discover that our technical civilization and our scientific system—born from the demands of pure research—today ultimately act to satisfy instincts and are nonetheless dependent on the economic element governed by a political power, in turn completely manipulated by the Obstructers of the human being.

✳✳✳

Instincts are the vivification of what is dead in us, just as the machine is the illusory bestowal of life to something that does not even exist as an organism—it being real only as a solidified abstraction, that is, as a physical symbol of abstract thought, useful where we move in the series of ephemera, which are the things of physical space—further symbols—unknown, as such.

There is no symbol that is not a sign or letter of a language that requires, more than a symbolic science, or a tradition, the art of directly perceiving the living element of which it is the vestment—regardless of the object's level of manifestation—as a sign being the contingent negation of the living content.

But the art of direct perception cannot be taught by traditionalist knowledge, because it demands to be learned within perception itself as it arises in immediate experience. The immediacy must be intuited, not passed over by means of interpretations previously acquired from a learned esotericist. It is the most difficult exertion, because it implies the perception of immediate thought. Therefore, each of us draws from the symbol what can be sought in the depths of our soul. What we know about the symbol, is meaningless.

***

To truly think, we must each be worthy of being a modern-day spiritual practitioner: not someone who reduces ancient asceticism to modern thought, as the traditionalist does unknowingly but, rather, one who resurrects the timeless spirit of ancient asceticism, by converting the thinking by which we immediately think at this time—namely, the thinking that has in its very movement the secret of the spiritual practice, *not in that which, as ascetic content, takes on form insofar as it is already made.*

To truly experience thought, we must arrive at sense-free thinking. To truly experience the life of the senses, we must gather within perceiving the supra-individual power of thinking.

We must have pure thought, pure perception. In certain moments, we must refrain "ourselves from willing" when we encounter a thought, or open up to a perception. But in this "not willing of ourselves," we operate according to a deeper will, which discloses the world's secret reality to us in the depths of thinking, in the depths of perceiving.

In perceiving, we do not have to think, because the thinking of creation flows to us through the sensory datum; just as it flows to us in pure thought. In both cases, we momentarily overcome the conditions of death, which the bone-nerve system entails in corporeality, to be the foundation of waking consciousness—not of our will, but of our thinking.

In reality, we do not will by means of the nervous system, but we think by means of it. Willing manifests in us through the metabolic/limb system, but we can will it within the life-forces of the blood-muscular system. We can will it consciously only by way of thinking. When thinking by means of the nervous system devoid of life, we draw thought, reflected and therefore lifeless. For this reason, thought can only transmit reflected mental pictures to the will, but (it can) *not act directly* on it or by means of it.

As we lack living will in thought, we can be free of nature to a certain degree. But we cannot realize such freedom, because we have no control over willing. We make use of willing by means of abstract thought. We draw from a power of life that we do not directly possess.

Conversely, lifeless thought reflected by the nervous system—not dominating but reflecting the vital-sensory element in forms of mental pictures and in conceptual order—does not notice how we translate into knowledge and into a systematic science what merely demands the instinctive being, the being of nature, which governs from the impenetrable area of willing.

Just as the normality of the bones is their mineral structure, so too, is the normality of the nervous system its lifeless being, but not so much as to become mineralized, it having to become a ductile vehicle of transcendent forces, which we cannot perceive until we draw them reflected as thought from cerebrality—as a spent mental picture by means of which we edify knowledge and organize life.

The struggle that the inner human being sustains in order to be, as an "I," corporeally alive, is actually a struggle against the nature that bears life. It is a struggle against death, that it nevertheless conducts by destroying life.

***

That of the earth which appears is not the earth, but its past.

Everything on earth that has passed, everything on the earth that enters into the ironclad mechanism of nature's laws, that is already made and rationally foreseeable, and therefore is projected into the soul as a value and sentiment of life, is the vehicle in which the Obstructers of the human being move.

In our passive dependence on sensations, we essentially bind ourselves with potentially free inner forces to a world of non-freedom, that is, to the needs of our own corporeal-psychic nature, which is a world already made, exhausted in itself, that awaits liberation and new movement from us.

The investigation of nature that does not come to distinguish, within perceptions, the inner living element from the merely sensory one, cannot become objective knowledge, because it is unaware of the continuous alteration of its own content—objective only in the aspect of its measurability, and as such abstracted from its own reality. Analogously, an inner life founded on altered sensory experience, cannot become aware of its own principle if it does not perceive the dependence of the physical support on the past.

The Obstructer takes hold of us and dictates our thoughts in what is predictable, rationalistic, necessary, automatic, habitual, and expressive of nature. In each already-made thought, which does not draw on its own pure source within its movement, we do not express our true being.

The Obstructer cannot act in the unpredictable, in the inner rising element, namely in what is not bound to the earthly processes of death. It cannot act in what is taken away from nature, in what does not depend on physical dynamisms—namely, in the autonomous thinking of human beings.

In autonomous thinking, an order higher than that of nature manifests.

Super-nature is that without which nature could not exist. Nature as an autonomous *quid* does not exist. Nevertheless, human self-consciousness begins to operate in place of a creative principle that it presumes to bear, abstractly, into the realm of nature. In this way, it eliminates in itself the possibility of really bearing it.

***

The forming of self-consciousness, out of a structural necessity, initially arrests within us the work of super-nature, which only until now has enabled us to evade animality—by forcing us to expel the animality that continuously tends to form in us through the persistent influence of earthliness.

At a later stage, which has now arrived, self-consciousness is actualized as an immediate form of super-nature. From this moment, the most dangerous period for humankind begins.

From the present epoch onwards, the human race risks producing an animal sub-race, or falling into animality, if the forces of self-consciousness, springing forth from the spirit, not recognizing itself in their principle—as should happen by way of an elevated logical consequentiality—are taken hold of by nature and, therefore, degraded.

The danger is that self-consciousness excludes the very principle from which it emanates, even while using its forces. In that case, the semblance of its freedom is manipulated by the Obstructer. Human degeneration acquires a systematic and normative power, through the very forces by means of which today they could begin to redeem themselves.

***

Nature is complete; the visible earth is the earth's past.

What is predictable, because it is already finished and scientifically pre-determinable, is necessarily mechanical. Its present-day symbol is the machine.

What is dead or continuously perishes, and expresses in us the past devoid of life, is the skeletal-nervous system.

The possibility of thinking arises from the spirit's tangency with the purely physical element of corporeality. It owes its very movement to the fact that it cannot be grasped by the vital process of the body, but it itself tends to be articulated in the vital (or etheric) body, there, where it does not serve the relationship of the "I" with the sensory and is, therefore, not extinguished in sensation or mental pictures.

Thought is born from being reflected in the least vital element of the organism. It can know the sensory world by immersing itself into the lifelessness of the earth, simply by limiting itself, or individualizing itself, or binding itself to the mineral element of the body.

In order to oppose and bind itself to the nervous system and to experience the world in its abstract physicality, thought leaves behind its own living being.

Yet the living being is immanent to thought, but its immanence, contradicting all human logic, is always transcendent. At one time, it was the light of life of the nervous system. Now, it is the light that is reflected in a nervous system devoid of life.

Thought—alive in its being—which gives itself but does not reveal itself as thinking, carries out a temporary experience of death in reflecting the sensory, the past of the earth—that of the earth which is dead.

By conferring to the earth's dead being an abstract correlation that feigns life, which is not its internal revivification but, rather, a projection of life into the lifeless, we unknowingly tend to reproduce the animal category, enucleating in itself form, through an unconscious surrender of itself to the collectivistic and mechanical entity—behind whose abstract organicity, the cosmic powers adverse to the human being urge.

***

Abstract organicity is visible in certain associations that call themselves initiatic and yet have the chrism of officialdom and the coloring of specific policies, supporting themselves on a ceremonialism for whose forms, under such conditions, no intuitive capacity can be given and on an apparently traditional symbolism, (both of) which only serve to feed, in the individual, a vague and unconscious mysticism. Such mysticism to varying degrees present today in every individual, is here an expression of an empirical "I" that tends to enjoy its own limitation and simultaneously persuade itself to overcome it by proceeding inexpensively along sacred and ritualistic paths.

The seriousness of being part of such associations does not consist so much in the associative fact, which has a humanly understandable value, and in some way positive, as in the unconscious cooperation in the forming of the occult soul amalgam, necessary, at its level of somnambulism, to the maneuver of the impersonal powers adverse to the human being.

The reality is that only an initiatic content could justify the existence of such associations—the inverse cannot occur.

***

Impersonal powers adverse to the human being already direct present-day culture, since this culture is a product of cerebralism, namely of thought in its formulation deprived of the force that renders its inner movement possible, including that of self-privation.

The self-destruction of thought requires force-thought in order to be accomplished. The result is the systematic degradation of this (force-thought) and the possibility that we draw structures from it adverse to its original nature.

The degradation of the force-thought is possible according to the conviction—which is now taken even when not suspected—that the brain produces thought, (a conviction) born in a moment of thought's impotence to have itself other than as a reflection. It is a moment that responds to a physio-psychic contingency that by being fixed in its precariousness, becomes a pathological condition. Such a condition, by becoming a doctrine and, therefore, by becoming known through the spirit's altered forces, acquires in these times a formative and ordering power.

The fact that the error of thinking and the destruction of its creative virtue are possible thanks to the very production of thought—to the extent that the Obstructer within us needs the spirit's force to exercise its power against the spirit—explains why such pseudo-teachers of today have access (up to a certain limit) to thought that is metaphysically reliable.

The metaphysical reliability of such expositors is possible only as a reflection that imitates the pre-reflected movement of thinking, by tending to give in an esoteric ceremonial and traditional guise—woven of a symbolism whose sense is now mute—premature forms of an occult order, which cannot be realized, since it can be impressed only as a mental picture within the soul oblivious of its own sensory ties—within the soul devoid of that imaginative spiritual practice that, for the disciple of today, is indispensable for freeing the inner element of life from the experience of the senses.

An occult order can only be established for the liberated "I"; but the "I" can become free only where its being manifests the greatest bond—in sensory consciousness—which can be eluded only by means of esoteric illusionism. The individual expression of the "I" is considered a form of luciferic pride by an Arabic type of metaphysics, (that has) penetrated Western circles to paralyze the spiritual research urgently needed at this time, while in reality such pride is precisely the one which suggests that the image of perfection be sought outside of one's own egoism, so that the ego is neither known, nor overcome. Rather it is strengthened.

3.

On Magical Perceiving

What in the present time appears inexplicable and, yet, can give a measure of the contradiction within science, is science's incapacity to turn its own investigation toward activities such as thinking and perceiving, which are also the sources of its knowing.

Along these lines, refined investigations undoubtedly exist. However, it must be said that, in spite of their regulatory analytical guise, they are devoid of the realism upon which they presume to base themselves, since they fail to apply the principle of the so-called "pure experience."

And those of us who are not asleep at this level, but want to see how effectively things are going, must ascertain that no serious scientific research proposes a pure experience of thinking and of perceiving. In fact, it is the experience that is carefully avoided, because it is subconsciously intuited as revealing the urgent need of a completely different orientation of culture and of technology, by demanding an objectivism of depth, with respect to which researchers at present are comfortably asleep. Such objectivism, among other things, would give rise to the subject of the experience, excluded from dogmatic empiricism and abstracted from philosophy as well as from psychology.

In a similar direction, scientific investigations continuously skip over, so to speak, the true subject, since they are aimed at the "already-perceived" (physiology of the brain, mechanism of sensation) and at the "already-thought" (psychological analysis and logic) by means of a perceiving and a thinking which, should (themselves) be examined. The criteria of pure experience is fully betrayed, because it appears inconceivable, extra-scholastic to modern-day scientists with regard to perceiving and thinking.

We would need to discover that realism is an error when we refer to immediate reality, but it becomes the vehicle of truth when the "immediate" is itself the mediation, in its purity—namely, pure perceiving, pure thinking.

***

The current of the "I" that flows unconscious in the blood, extinguishes its force in sensation as well as in mental picturing, to provide the lifeless content necessary to reflected consciousness.

Such a current can be recognized as the element of life that makes perceiving and thinking possible, independently of the moment of reflectivity necessary to consciousness. In this element of life, the ordinary power of human beings is present, unconsciously, as the *possibility* to penetrate and have control over the sensory—never realized as such, given its supra-sensory nature. *We humans effectively operate as supra-sensory beings, but for now we can recognize ourselves only in the sensory manifestation.* Therefore, we see only the world's sensory realm.

The function of perceiving and of thinking is not what appears to present-day science; their content is true not in itself, but as a means to activate an individual willing that, usually, in a non-conscious area, meets with the current of extra-individual willing. This (current) within the human being operates by opposing the spirit, if it is not interpenetrated with "thinking will," or with exerted forces of the consciousness soul, which today is the severe problem of morality, made incomprehensible by the dialecticism prevalent in dual form—materialistic and spiritual. Because the strongest willing that we are capable of realizing today, depends completely on instincts. For this reason, instincts are about to constitute the foundation of the present civilization.

The element of life of the "I" continuously expresses itself as a current of will. But it is a will that we use, without possessing. It is the supra-sensory that we encounter only in sensory effects.

Our human willing is longing, of ourselves and the world; but as longing, it only manifests in its "inhering" to the cerebral system.

Willing becomes longing as a human expression, centered on cerebralism.

Willing, which manifests in the soul as the sentient force and in the organism as the structural and motor force, turns into longing in becoming the vehicle of the reflected "I." Its power of impersonality is corrupted in becoming a personal fact, but it must become a personal fact, in order for the corruption to be known and confronted.

The task of the "I" is to will itself as an individual entity, so as to express the power of impersonality, which is its foundation. Normally, in fact, each of us wills not as an individual, but as a corporeal being, to which we each actually refer when we say "I." We should look for who truly says "I": whether suffering or rejoicing, whether thinking or willing.

Willing's relationship with cerebralism continuously takes place by way of thinking and sensory perception, but it is never experienced, since the being of consciousness knows of itself in the "perceived" and the "already-thought." The "I" does not experience the sensory world. Meanwhile, there is no experience that does not have it as a subject. It is the subject that exists, but excluded.

By means of perceiving and thinking, therefore, the occurrence of longing is inevitable. But likewise its overcoming is possible, where we stop ignoring what happens in the process of perceiving and thinking. All human error asks for this knowledge. It is the error that takes place in order for this knowledge to emerge.

By going beyond the current schemes of physiology and of psychology, we must be able to gather directly, within perceiving and thinking, the volitional element of life, which is corrupted as a vehicle of egoic consciousness. It is not a question of "unconscious" or subconscious but, rather, of actualizing a higher state of consciousness in which we are already active. It is not a matter of diminishing but, rather, of strengthening waking consciousness.

***

What we normally perceive is not the living being, but rather the dead being of the earth. Yet we believe to perceive even what we simply presume to be alive, having momentary life in perceiving, without being a perception to us.

Seeing only physical notes, sensory aspects, material phenomena of the world, we can only establish numerical, chemical and mechanical relationships between them. But we do not notice that they are relationships of thought, namely of the force that alone can be related. We give the semblance of life to a life that is foreign to us. We create the civilization of the machine. We interpret the world through dialectics, and do not escape such dialectics even when we believe we grasp the obscurity and the narrowness of this world.

The fact that thinking undergoes an affinity to the dis-animation of the cerebral substance, makes it such that, in its impotence, it is grasped by the vital processes of the nervous system. Such processes—not being dominated in cerebralism by consciousness—express instinctive forces, to which thought is able to conform or not able to conform, without however having any power over them.

The world of instincts would not be able to have anything on us, if we were not grasped by it in the cerebral system, due to the fact that the vital processes that are ruled by the spirit in the remaining organism, can only be ruled in cerebralism by the spirit during sleep. But in such dominion, we are not present as beings endowed with consciousness.

Our current task (as spiritual practitioners) can be understood in this sense. We provide the soul with its original forces, through the intensification of thought, leading the cerebral organ to a stillness that is equivalent to sleep, while remaining awake. We encounter thought in its living moment, whose reality is not to depend on the nervous system. It is a moment or state in which we sleep as ordinary individuals, because thought manifests where we as conscious beings are awake.

Normally, by entering sleep we lose the consciousness that only lights up through the cerebral organ's opposition to the inner life. When we are awake, the spirit does not live as consciousness in the corporeal processes but, rather, in the system of representations that arises by reflecting itself in a part of such processes—the nervous-cerebral one.

For this reason, the life of human beings today is contradictory. It is an illness from which we cannot be cured, if we fail to notice how only recently have we drawn conscious life, *completely*, from the cerebral support: so that we no longer have the possibility of inspiration, in art or in thought.

All that we vaguely intuit of the spiritual beyond the sensory, is not an achievement beyond the current condition of dependence on the nervous system but, rather, an echo in us of a psychic non-cerebral being, which more and more goes on changing, more and more being destined to corrupt itself, and to intoxicate the soul, if we fail to recognize its function, that is, if we do not recognize how it can be restored under the sign of consciousness—certainly not of dialectical consciousness, certainly not by means of psychoanalysis.

***

Despite the content of perception, it nonetheless gives itself to the "I" by means of a physiological process with which it objectively has nothing to do, since this process is simply a conductor. Just like a tube that conducts water has no other relationship with it.

This point should be fundamental for modern physiology, which naively seeks perception in its corporeal vehicle rather than in the perceptive act itself, whose substance is real in its incorporeal moment, which only a strengthened consciousness can distinguish from the moment of its corporeal inherence.

The investigation of the perceptive act, in fact, can only be self-experience. To carry it out it apart from ourselves means to believe we can have perceptions other than our own. When such an act can be observed in ourselves, an investigation of nature begins, which already as such is the overcoming of its limit. We connect with a current of life that can be recognized even outside ourselves, in other beings and in the world, as an objectivity independent of sensory means, even if it manifests by means of them. An investigation of the sensory that does not arrive at that possibility, once physical-mathematical knowledge of the world is achieved, cannot proceed beyond the position of primitive realism. It confuses measurability with function, the physical datum with the force that manifests by means of this datum.

In reality, whenever physiological processes inhere to perceptive contents, influencing other corporeal systems, you have states of illness. Even a mental illness is this, and it can clothe itself with much logic.

* * *

When we perceive the movements of the limbs, or our own emotions, the objects of the world, or our own thoughts, this—along the lines of objective bodily mediation—occurs thanks to the encounter of a process between the nerves and the circulatory system, to which a subconscious breathing process responds.

Nevertheless, the perception of thinking, possible thanks to the mediation of the cerebral organ, is the one which demands the minimal cooperation of the circulatory system. It demands this cooperation for as much as is necessary for the purposes of an exclusion of its vital element, when thinking tends to be autonomous and highly logical.

The more vital the thought, the less vitality it draws from the cerebral organ: the less the blood determines the type of thought. Rather, thought, rising up again as light from dialectical remains, begins to operate within the current of the blood. And the more essentially it operates there, the less conscious it is of this operation, all its consciousness being directed to the content for which it lives as thought. This is the secret of those who meditate.

In that case, the brain begins to have a relationship with the blood that cooperates in its autonomy, that is, it does not oppose its possibility of immobility.

In profound meditation, the circulatory system's cooperation with the nervous system is related to the possibility for the brain to implement its profound non-entity—its incorporeal force again becoming positive.

Wherever the paths of the blood and the paths of the nerves meet, a breathing process is always had, in which the feeling of a given nature emerges. The subconscious breath cannot help but express the corporeal need and the subtle instinctive world.

But the process is reversible. The conscious silence of cerebralism is an act of will that brings us to that independence from the breath, by which only the quality of breath can be transformed.

***

We are able to perceive thanks to the concurrence of the conscious mental element with an unconscious vital-volitional current, which knows no separation between subject and object and therefore participates in the living substance of the world. We are unaware of this (living substance) in perceiving, despite accepting it, since our acceptance of it, in becoming conscious, is each time the act that extinguishes it.

Of this life current, as much becomes deadened as becomes conscious experience, so that it can arise as a mental picture or sensation.

Perception is deprived of its light by the individualizing demand of consciousness. The necessity of the reflected "I" paralyzes the world's living element from being able to be directly perceived by the "I."

The process of life that lies at the heart of perception and without which perception would not be, has as much reality as escapes consciousness. In effect, for consciousness to be egoic consciousness, it loses reality in perceiving, having only its immediate vestment. It has the reflection of the world, not the world.

Matter, which seems to exist, is appearance. This suggests a foundation within it, whose *nonexistence*, truly renders it objective like matter. And this is the everyday contradiction or illusion of human beings, who assume as real that from which they have removed the foundation: not knowing they are thinking it.

Thus, appearance, assumed as real in sensation and in mental picturing, moves feeling and willing. It alters the life of the soul.

***

By way of sensory experience, a part of the soul is confined to live and be exalted for what is essentially not real, while the other participates by virtue of deep impersonal forces in what is real in the act of perceiving.

In a profound part of the soul, a truth thickens, which we are incapable of experiencing with normal consciousness, because this (consciousness), as egoic consciousness, opposes it. In the soul, a memory is thus formed of reality and of the living beyond sensory appearing, which, unable to manifest, will come to pass after death.

Nonetheless, for us as disciples, a spiritual practice of memory today is possible, which can lead us to rediscover within ourselves the true substance of our lives—namely, the one from which is woven the "body of memory" that we ordinarily experience after death.

Through the emergence of true memory, we can open up to the profound value of human relations and to the cosmic resonance of events and encounters from which life is woven, without the necessity of death, so that we can understand its meaning, so that we can know all the oppositions to the light, the individualistic and worldly tensions, the misery of physically possessing things, (the misery) of envy and of ingratitude, bound to the hypnosis of abstract sensory perception—abstract because it is removed from the possibility of perceiving what makes the sensory real.

***

Perceiving is always an act of the "I," therefore (it is) non-physical, mediated by a physical process.

Sensory perception, like the perception of a sentiment or of an impulse or that of a thought, is always an inner act. It is always the same motion of the "I," now turned to a sensory content, now to a non-sensory content. Sensory mediation is always for a non-sensory event—in sensory form. However, the form itself is in itself non-sensory.

This motion of the "I" bears the consciousness of the "I," but it is unconscious of itself.

Our art as spiritual practitioners is to take hold of ourselves in this movement aroused by the sensory (realm), because it is the same through which we will be able to penetrate a non-sensory content—it having been initially aroused by sensory perception.

Through the will, we can only experience, as an initial supra-sensory life, what has been aroused as a conscious movement of the sensory. Such is the sense of our life on earth.

The meaning of sense experience is precisely its ability to awaken (within the sensory vestment) a movement whose supra-sensory nature we must recognize, without which sensory perception would not be possible. In truth, the senses do not experience the sensory.

***

It is necessary to observe without having thoughts, because true thinking—the most alive—is active in this observing. But it is the art of who fully possesses rationality, so as to be able to have it at will, in a single pure moment, in perceiving.

What we observe is always a thought in which we are immersed. It is a matter of knowing that we are observing.

Original thinking, full of life, flows in the calm "observing of the world," without thoughts.

Living thinking encounters world thought alive in perception, which ordinarily is given continuously as a life, which is lost, because it is believed to be grasped.

Life, so as to not be lost, must not be grasped. It has no need of being grasped. It is within us, connected in the depths with the world substance. Through ordinary sensory perception, we unknowingly encounter the surfacing of such depths within us, which manifest because they are clothed in the unconscious light of thinking, within perceiving.

We must notice this thinking—which is present in each of us who perceives through the senses—as a sign of high rank. The mistake is in fact not to notice the light that flows within perceiving, not to know that of which we make use and without which we would not have perception.

To look at the world, to perceive the world, is the most important function carried out along the lines of self-consciousness by the being that that inhabits the earth. For it is the thinking most alive, the still uncertain outline of magical thinking. The most awakened consciousness still sleeps in the life of perceptions and mistakes its dream, its knowing, its esotericism for reality. It escapes the thinking where it begins to awaken itself, because it loves its illusory expression. It identifies with it.

We must not escape nascent thinking, because everything that can flow to us as a power of life, is urgently needed in the spirit's encounter with the sense world.

Only a proud spiritualism, inspired by the forces adverse to us, tends to grasp, prematurely, a supra-sensory order conserved in traditional images, symbols and rituals, by avoiding or presuming to transcend thought born of sense experience, which it considers an impediment to the implementation of such an order. It tries to deprive us of the sense of experience of the physical world in which we activate the nascent forces of the "I," thanks to which we can overcome evil and error on earth.

The experience of the senses escapes both the materialism of science, as well as spiritualism and traditionalism. Meanwhile, it is the experience through which we can grasp the forces of egoity, as fallen forces of the "I." Only the ego identified and experienced can offer that for which we are on earth—the transformation of the ego.

***

There is no need to think, when we contemplate the warmth or the form or the light of a tree, because all that can be thought is already present before our gaze, as an image. We must only perceive that of it which we already take in as form and movement.

We must give ourselves to this image with the same power of abandonment that renders its immediate perception possible. There is no interruption between perception and image; rather there is identity, which is the magical imagining's power of self-giving to perceiving.

If the separative egoism of the sense organs had not been won, for which every human being is given to have objective perceptions, the identity between the sensory world and the self-giving of imagining (from which perception is born) would be impossible. In fact, we perceive so that what is already united— of us and of the world— can reveal itself.

We are still dormant before this revelation.

In sensory perceiving, egoism has been won by the Logos. Our human task is to realize within ourselves the extinction of egoism already implemented in the sense organs and in their communion with the world. But, for this reason, we must pay pure attention to certain sensory experiences. We must practice having pure perceptions, untainted by instantaneous judgment or psychism.

Sensory perception is already the union of the spirit with the world. We must notice this union because it takes place at the locus of consciousness. By virtue of contemplation it becomes a conscious communion. This is the task of our free being.

It is pure perception, the rediscovery of the power of abandonment that uproots fear in the depths.

In reality, we never abandon ourselves to what we perceive, because we do not know that it gives itself for the abandonment. We ignore its giving, for the secret fear of being abandoned, for the unconscious aversion to the spirit that comes to meet us and to the life that would want to unite itself to consciousness. Because lifeless consciousness is the error, which has become the habit that we are afraid to abandon.

Therefore, we think according to an inner process in which we participate, but unconscious, whose fulfillment we do not want to know, since we are satisfied with what we directly see, consider, make dialectical, measure, translate into number and weight. Culture is born from the inability to receive the "living" in both nature and history.

What is perceived is immediately converted into egoic sensation and this governs mental picturing and limits thinking. The perceived becomes something other than what it actually is, and its alteration rises up as reality.

All that is seen, all that is perceived and not experienced as a power of image arising from perception, is unreal as soon as it is translated into sensation and mental pictures—*being real only in the perceptual moment,* which we still do not have the strength or the wisdom to grasp in its objectivity.

***

We do not need to think except in a preliminary way what, as living nature, turns out to be the form of an extra-human thought. If we as thinkers train ourselves to open up to the inner element of the very thinking that thinks and if we are each able to stand as the contemplator before the objective force of thought, we can come to contemplate in the sensory world our own thinking (as) one with the living thinking of the world's entities. We have no need, except contingently, to reconstruct this thinking dialectically. Through contemplation, we must only allow such thinking to manifest its structuring power and its meaning within the soul, which it can later express in dialectical thought.

Analogously, physicists do not interpret or dialecticize an experiment before it unfolds objectively before them. The attention by means of which they follow such an experiment is more important than the interpretation, because in the attention the intuitive motion of interpreting is already in progress.

4.

The Essence of Meditating

The "I" as a spiritual entity is articulated in the blood, but it cannot help but be dormant within the blood. It can flow there as long as it receives the dormancy of minerality, by binding itself to the mineral entity of the blood, to permeate it with life.

In fact, the conscious form of the "I" does not spring from the blood, but from the nerve structure, functionally opposed to that of the blood. It springs from a structure whose minerality does not draw life directly from the "I," but from the system in which the "I" is expressed directly—namely, the blood-metabolic one.

In the blood, the spirit is the power of life. In the nervous system it is devoid of life, being only reflected. It is the form of the contingent "I."

In the system of the brain, the spirit is able to flow and within a certain limit arise as a conscious determination. Meanwhile, within the blood, it is present as a metaphysical force, but unconscious. By means of the nervous system, the spirit can flow to the extent that it transcends the peculiar physical structure. Meanwhile, in the blood it is incarnated, or immanent, but, as such, immersed in deep sleep.

Flowing dormant in the blood, the "I" is the bearer of nature. It carries this nature with the force that it possesses as a spiritual entity. For this reason, wherever it encounters its conscious form, it becomes a force of the ego. It is longing.

The metaphysical path of the blood can only be found by the "I," which, having aroused self-consciousness by means of the cerebral support, that is, by means of a system opposed to what allows it to incarnate, knows how to free itself from the support and thus from the impulsive influence of the blood through the acquisition of self-consciousness.

Such an influence is the alteration of the force of the "I," but, in its lower nature, it really belongs neither to the "I" nor to the blood. It rises from the blood, but it materializes in the brain. Here, the blood, as a current that bears the spirit, encounters its own inverse force and assumes its sign, simultaneously prevailing over it, insofar as it is endowed with a life that such a force is lacking—given that consciousness is reflected.

The animal forms that tend to rise up in the head for the time being as modes of conceiving or as mental impulses, are possible because of the reduction to abstractness of the current of thinking, whose profound life is the same for which the "I" flows in the blood and expresses itself cerebrally as ego.

Through this flow devoid of the life forces of consciousness, longing flows in the blood as fire that continuously lights up from the sensory contents rendered extraneous to their supra-sensory substance along the path of the nerves. The ego opposes the "I."

Therefore, abstract thought indirectly nourishes longing and arouses animal forms, against which thought's profound forces have to continuously struggle. Without such forces, not even abstract thought would be possible.

***

The pure forces of thought, to realize their depth, need to retrace the paths of the blood system. Only pure thinking can penetrate an instinct with authority, by possessing its inner force.

The perceiving in which the spirit finds its own movement of life and the thinking that draws from its own spiritual source, open the paths to the "I" in the flowing of the blood.

In the paths of the blood, the "I" rediscovers its ancient being and turns toward the seat of the heart, which is the human-terrestrial base of its celestial power.

Without the empty stillness of the brain, achieved according to the spiritual practice of thinking, the "I" continuously undergoes, as the life of the soul, the influence of its inverse force, there, where it manifests as waking consciousness.

Cerebral immobility and its emptiness are the opening to the Divine, or to the transmuting forces of human substance. For the spiritual practitioner, they are the independence from the mental (sphere) and therefore from corporeality and, at the same time, the identity of the "I" with its principle, outside of the soul's creative currents and in harmony with them. This achievement is not an abstract evasion, but the possibility of encountering the incorporeal light within perceptions, or within pure thinking, the being of the life that continuously flows from the world by means of the senses and from internal thinking, but is continuously corrupted by the necessity of the ego.

With everyday perceiving and thinking, we today unconsciously provide continuous nourishment to longing. We achieve the conscious moment—sensory and dialectical—by the fact that the supra-sensory content of the object is taken away from us by limiting forces. We notice the object only through its physical projection, by means of perception and mental picturing. Each ideal valuation receives its imprint of non-truth.

The error always becomes more immediate to human perceiving and thinking, with the gradual accentuation of our self-consciousness. Nevertheless, we—who once in our sensorial-rational experience were protected by the wisdom of the Tradition—today realize, by means of it, an element of freedom by virtue of which we can regain what was taken from us—namely, the living element of perceiving, the living element of thinking.

Certainly, there is no self-initiation, but an individual work of preparation of the instruments of knowledge—which uniquely depends on the initiative of disciples and leads, by way of their decisions, to the threshold of the supra-sensory—cannot be avoided.

**

By means of the brain, the soul sinks into the earthly (realm), because the brain is the vehicle of earthliness within the human structure.

The cerebral organ has become materialized and refined, to be the most subtle substance for the spirit's encounter with the physical cosmos, that is, the instrument of depth projection of the spirit into mineral determinacy—from which thinking at last is born.

The spirit is in the physical world, but dormant. It is awake where it does not manifest physically.

In cerebralism, the spirit—awake only by means of its reflection—experiences the dormancy of matter; yet it does not know it as sleep but, rather, as reality.

The soul enters into materiality by means of the cerebral organ, in the same way that the formative force of the plant is connected with the earth's profound energies by means of the roots.

The threshold toward the physical world, pursued inversely, is the threshold of the spiritual world.

Those of us who only know the direction of cerebralism, indeed perceive the earthly, but cannot know the earth, because in the perceptive act we unconsciously lose the forces that penetrate and dominate the earth. They are the forces that render perceiving possible, flowing as currents of life that consciousness extinguishes in order to arise.

Thus the physical world is not known. And this is the reason for which the spiritual world cannot be known. Yet, for this reason, dialectics is capable of talking about it inexhaustibly.

Dialectics is the sign of the impotence of humans to penetrate the real world of matter and, thus, the world of the spirit.

In reality, matter does not exist outside of the spirit.

***

By limiting ourselves to knowledge that comes to us from the cerebral direction, we deprive ourselves of the possibility to know what operates through cerebralism. We only think what we are led to think by the tangency with the cerebral vehicle, without being able to have thought in its real movement and to to conceive such a movement. As if the plant were limited to being a root and did not have the root as a means of building its own form out of the earthly (realm).

Thought is an abstract outline of a form; therefore it is an incomplete process, arrested in its emergence. In wanting to be valued as such, it opposes the formative force out of which it arises.

As a threshold to the sensory, the brain is the threshold to the spiritual world—namely, the threshold that one must cross.

The threshold becomes impassable insofar as it is unknown. We must experience the dead state of the cerebral system, to know the darkness that separates humanity from its foundation.

Knowledge is only that which leads to glimpsing in the "threshold" the experience of annihilating an architecture of illusory human values, rendered necessary by the worthiness of the support of human consciousness. The implementation of consciousness, beyond the darkness of support, can give rise to the true being of the world.

The threshold is the limit to the human, the boundary of exteriority that arises as objective, the sign of the intellect's separation from reality.

All that which is mediated by the brain, from the most noble thought to longing, from the most spiritual representations to the functions of nature, has nothing to do with the spirit, even if it manifests through the forces of the spirit. We actually ignore such forces.

Through the brain, the soul is immersed in the earthly (realm), not in order to forget itself in it, as normally happens, but to know depth as the depth of its own strength.

***

Head thinking is not true thinking. But we do not arrive at the intelligence of the heart, without knowing how this intelligence binds to cerebralism to become reasoning, from which we inevitably move.

The thinking of the head is not the spirit, but its conscious embryonic surfacing. Therefore, it is only the outline of thought. True thinking is still not thought by us, since we do not have the breath for it, since we cannot sustain it. In fact, only to the degree in which it opposes the spirit as a reflecting screen, can the cerebral apparatus arouse the spirit's conscious activity, initially as a simple response to the opposition.

In every other area of the organism, the spirit has only a contingent opposition in the mineral element. Such opposition is necessary to the architecture of the body and to the vital equilibrium. Therefore, it is continuously resolved by the spirit through the rhythmic activity of its formative forces, unless it has to do with a sick area, namely with an area where the oppositional relation is altered, directly or indirectly, by the uncontrolled mental-cerebral opposition.

There exist no formative forces that are not supra-sensory. Their activity in the organism is compromised by excess or defect of the sensory element. Only the form's destructive forces, and not the formative forces, belong to the sensory sphere.

The spirit operates as life. It begins to operate as thought, there, where the life it edifies opposes it in a well-defined organ—namely, the brain.

Wherever the opposition does not arouse the life of thought, and with that the thinking autonomy, life as an animal force makes use of thought's power of form.

***

What is merely physiological can take hold of the life of the soul to the extent that it begins to rise to a mental value.

The true force of the human being is not the "mental"; it is not cerebralism. Our art is to overcome our worth as mental beings, to overcome the animal forms with which the head system tends to spiritually reproduce or to project our state of physical determination, which has become, in modern times, a mental value.

Our art is to overcome what binds us to the bodily processes of the head, so as to one day encounter the order of forces that edified it.

It is the order of forces that continues to edify the thoracic zone and the limbs, where we are immersed in the flow of cosmic currents, unknowingly, because we know about ourselves only in the head—there, where we are excluded from this flow.

The human head is complete. What exists in our organism beyond the head, beyond the nervous system, is moving towards its fulfillment. We can say that outside of the head, we are immersed in the rhythm of stellar forces. In an unconscious "area," we participate in such a rhythm, but we can consciously participate there, by an indirect path, with what we manage to will in the head independently of our physiological processes and of the anti-rhythmic forces of our own instinctive being.

According to the Master of the new times*, the past lies in the human head, the future in the limbs.

It is the future where we cooperate to the extent that we perceive what allows us to be conscious thanks to our dependence on the physical mediation of the head—which is our dependence on nature.

***

Nature is the species. The human species is the tangency with the animal world.

The tangency is the provisional identity. We do not have to fall in love with the functions of nature which are the signs of the "fall," but only use them, cognitively, distinguishing the life of the soul from them. The less soul we bind to the functions of nature, the more such functions realize their autonomy and express the vital balance in which the spirit operates.

The human being is not the species, but the individuality that assumes the vestment provided to it by the species, to express itself as a spiritual being in the earthly realm.

Our human origin is not the animal. On the contrary, animality is the unresponsive substance that humanity eliminates so as to elaborate the form necessary for our earthly experience.

That the form of the species dominates the soul—to the extent that it identifies with natural functions—is the inversion of the task for which we are on earth. In this way, animality is not redeemed but ennobled through the intellect, as happens today with culture put into motion worldwide in order to serve the species, not the human being; because nature as a species can express itself only in the mental-cerebral (sphere), by assuming the vestment of thought, the force of individuality—making what belongs to the spirit its own.

Cerebral human beings, human beings of the head, human beings that go organizing culture and civilization by means of the head forces, unconsciously tend to reconstitute humanity as an animal species on earth. They tend to fix it in animal nature—which does not belong to them—and to make, out of the spirit, an instrument of that dominion.

---
*   Rudolf Steiner

This tendency can be recognized in the various aspects of a reconstitution of "group souls"—namely, the resurgence of ethnic myths and of race struggles, the reinvigoration of political obsessions, the epileptoid unleashing of enthusiastic or irate madman/women, the mechanization of mass attitudes, anonymous societies, the collective subjection to advertising suggestions.

The everyday animalization of the human being becomes a scientific and technical fact. The life of the soul is grasped by the needs of physical corporeality, interpreted tastefully and justified by science. No intellectual activity can escape it.

There is a psychology, Freudian or analytical, that provides an inner background to this situation, not because it manages to see it from the outside, but because it belongs to it. And it demonstrates this with the empiricism of its own method that ascends, with unconscious automatism, to dogmatic dignity. Such psychology exhibits no suspicion of the background implicit in its own investigation. If by chance this psychology succeeded in seeing it, it would inevitably behold the sense of its own analysis disappear. This analysis in fact operates as the very expression of that psychic background. It begins by unconsciously identifying with what it would like to penetrate. The phenomenon itself has become psychology, endowed with the necessary logic to cultivate, in the form of therapy, the illness that it presumes to have individuated.

Likewise, spiritual vocations, Yoga, Zen, traditional paths, neo-occultisms are attitudes today adversely affected by the unawareness of their inevitable move from cerebralism. They operate towards a spiritual legitimation of animality, since they ignore the soul's occult dependence on the cerebral support. And yet they lack the art of converting the vision of the absolute otherness of nature and of history, due today to the integral dominion of reflected thought.

No traditional doctrine exists that can teach present-day researchers how the dependence of thought on cerebralism and the key for it not to be dependent, take place.

The thinking that thinks, whatever its object, as reflected thought, is the dependence. Whatever the research, the intuition, the meditation, it moves from cerebralism and therefore from animality—namely from the soul bound to corporeality. Thus, in this initial movement lies the possibility of its positive direction.

Animality is not the structure of the brain, nor the series of forces that are dormant in it, but the subordination of consciousness to what should only be its support. This support is not known as such. Its reality is not experienced, but deduced. No one sees how thinking is reflected by the cerebral organ. To see it, we need to be outside of reflectivity—what no psychology or physiology has yet the possibility to experience.

***

Thought's relationship with the cerebral system is an unknown relationship, which for now we can only imagine and consider logically, by means of thinking bound to such a system. Meanwhile, abysmally far from an awareness of it is any investigation of a physiological order that pretends to grasp it within the cerebral organ—like someone who seeks the source of water within the metal of a pipe.

Thinking, insofar as it thinks, is already the product of the relationship between the original thinking-force and the cerebral system, so that any dialectical or psychic provision that presumes to remove the soul's dependence on egoic nature, inevitably expressing itself as thought that thinks and adjusting precisely to what (in a presumed form) it has thought, is essentially in its fundamental nature, dependent on nature. It does not escape nature. Nature becomes spiritualism.

Only investigators who *overcome* thought can do something along those lines, namely those capable of finding the lost thinking, who really possess thinking, so as to be able to extinguish its dialectical form with the very force by means of which they allow it to rise. In fact, there is no way to escape thought, except by possessing it without residues.

The force with which a thought is born, the force with which it is nourished and can be kept alive before us, is something more than the thinking with which we give form to a sensory or intellectual subject.

It is the force with which we know how to logically and clearly think, insofar as thought is dedicated to worldly things and to the concepts of things, according to a logical order. This order is to be possessed so that it can be overcome. Therefore, we must experience its inverse motion, since we only have its motion in an expressive direction.

The movement of thinking is to be inverted. Thought that thinks, thought that intuits, thought that meditates is not complete unless it draws on itself. It must be inverted; it must lead back to the point in which it has not yet closed itself in form and therefore is not yet lifeless. Only then does it reveal what it is, manifesting itself as the force of truth.

Essential truths are born as thought in the struggle against that which is habitual thinking.

Habitual thinking is thought that is unfree, abstract and dialectical—namely, thought that reflects or imitates truth, but is adverse to truth, because it no longer allows movement to thought, having become more important than it, as if it came from a source other than the thinking capable of thinking it.

The movement of thought is to be inverted, so that it can be the original light, which can again shine for humanity. But it is to be inverted not insofar as it is closed in form and abstract—which would generate more abstractness with a different sign—but, rather, as thinking in movement. *Thinking is to be inverted, not the already thought.*

Thought must think; it must intuit, it must meditate. But to escape its own reflected state, it must be able to invert its own movement. Within the movement of thought lies the principle of its creative resurgence. We must move the force-thought in the very movement aroused through reflectivity. The movement grasped is the principle of the redemption of thinking—the art of meditation.

The thinking of the present-day investigator must possess, non-dialectically, the whole process of logic, in its concluded connectivity, so as to gather within itself that which it continuously gives up by means of logic and that logic cannot contain.

We must invert the movement of thought, not what we have thought and cannot help but think. To think the already-thought backwards can be for us a preparation for the effective inversion of the movement, which is the inversion of reflectivity—the restitution of the light, namely the concrete sense of the spiritual practice of thinking.

***

In being reflected, thought ceases to be conditioned by the essence from which it springs. In fact, it becomes conscious in the sphere of bodily opposition to the spirit. But, therein, an a-nomy (*non-adherence to norms) follows, which is the possibility of freedom—but not freedom.

Instead, in ancient humans thought reflected the essence. It could not, nor did it need to oppose the essence. Ascetics did not have the problem of *freedom,* but of *liberation* from the human. Meanwhile, the task is the realization of the human. The problem of freedom arose because of reflected thought, when it ceased to be the vestment of the essence and began to operate as a formative element of consciousness, correlated to the logic of the exclusive earthly experience.

In spiritual practitioners of this time, the movement of thinking realizes the possibility of freedom, if it actualizes itself independently of the vital processes of the cerebral apparatus. In that case, the essence permeates thought and frees it of reflectivity. Thus, no longer "outside," but "within" waking consciousness, the identity of thought and its essence is realized.

The vital processes of the head do not belong to the brain substance, operating in it to sustain what it is insofar as it is organically complete. To the extent that it is organically complete, the head bears the imprint of transcendent forces of the cosmos. But it is in itself devoid of life. It draws life from other corporeal systems.

Being devoid of life, it is the substance through which the spirit, by way of a process of consciousness, arrives at the boundaries of physicality, allowing this (physicality) to grasp a part of itself—in reflected form, by means of which it arises as an egoic entity, whose structure no human logic can re-ascend. Yet, by virtue of the cerebral support, thinking human beings have the power to estrange themselves from corporeal nature and to establish a conscious relationship with the world.

This initial freedom of ours, this initial way of ours to be independent of corporeality, is merely a reflection of the essence.

It is still abstractness. Therefore, it undergoes the conditions of nature from which it tends to free itself.

The spirit as thought rejects, within cerebralism, the spirit as life. In opposing nature, the spirit's conscious activity must eliminate life.

From this elimination, deeper life forces are aroused, through a re-edification process. But it is always life that, making itself felt, cannot but oppose the spirit and that, therefore, the spirit must continuously destroy—until the death of the body.

From the opposition, the consciousness of the "I" that, as such, is opposed to the "I," essentially arises. But it is the opposition through which the "I" grasps the egoic nature in the depths.

Life's opposition to the spirit is, in effect, disease. In the brain, therefore, a disease of the soul—which has become organic—or an organ that lives off such disease can be seen. Such an organ, formed by way of sensory experience, as an alteration of an original spiritual organ, awaits healing by what humans are in essence, not by what, as dialectics, expresses the alteration itself.

**

Except for the skeletal system, the only system in the human organism not permeated with spiritual forces is the nervous system, because it is the only one not truly alive. For this reason, it can be the vehicle of the spirit. It is akin to the skeletal system, namely to the mineral element.

The earthly mineral, insofar as it is not permeated with life forces, is endowed with formative forces "outside" of its own corporeal being. Its corporeality is the negative of the spirit. Its interiority is its physical non-being.

Every physical body, as such, is the negation of the spirit, but in the pure mineral the negation is form itself. In the mineral devoid of life, the spirit has its place.

Matter must be devoid of life so that the spirit can flow through it freely. This can indicate what the spirit requires of the cerebral organ by means of consciousness.

The mineral is the world that in its pure existence bears the life of the spirit, because it does not embody it, but simply symbolizes it, being objectively "outside" it. The mineral exists only in negating the being that is its foundation. As minerality, it is pure appearance; with its flow in the form, it becomes the appearance proper to the physical-sensory aspect of the various levels of earthly being.

The mineral is the true void, because it does not grasp the spirit; it does not let it exist: it allows it to flow through itself. Therefore, *thinking touches, within cerebral minerality, the possibility of freedom.*

The substance of the nervous system, only insofar as it reflects the spirit as thought, is opposed to the spirit; but this opposition is virtual.

Akin to the mineral world, tending toward minerality, the nerve substance is actually such that the spirit is left free; the spirit passes through this substance without inhering.

This flow of the spirit is not conditioned by thought. It is the process punctually proceeding dialectics, unknown and yet immanent to thought. But, therefore, the task of thinking is to know the spirit's unconditionality, as a foundation.

Our freedom is virtual. We do not yet realize it. Since the nerve substance does not live a spiritual life, the spirit can manifest itself through it. We think. But the thinking that we can know is not the flow of the spirit through the nervous system but, rather, the reflection. The reflection is the inversion.

The inversion must be there, so that we can one day perceive it and, by perceiving it, know our own fall and the principle of its resurgence.

Thinking cannot be but reflection, since we do not draw immediate life from the spirit, but from the body. Thus, we draw consciousness not from the spirit, but from the reflection. Beyond this limit, our consciousness is lost. We do not possess the spirit that nevertheless flows to us through the nervous system, because in this flow we lie with our new consciousness, immersed in degrees of dream and profound sleep.

***

Not drawing life from the spirit, but from the body edified by the spirit, we receive the impulses of feeling and willing not from their sphere, but through the nervous system, that is, as reactions of a corporeal life bound to the sensory. In instinctive feeling and willing, we lose as a possibility of the waking state the flow of the spirit, which presents itself in its inversion.

We could rise to the awareness of this flow if we would come to meet the incorporeal forces of feeling and willing; but we know these forces corporally as sensations, that is, to the extent that they inhere to the nervous system. We have them as feelings and impulses, signifying something insofar as they are unconsciously furnished with thought. Without the vestment of thought, they could not become mental facts.

Instinctive feeling and willing can grasp thought, as reflection. They arise in consciousness, dominating it, because consciousness does not penetrate them.

We do not live in the spirit's direct movement, since we can only have its reflection. Therefore, we are forced to undergo the life of the nervous system, where, through the flow of the blood, forces of instinctivity continuously alter the light of thinking. We think by means of the alteration. Yet, the unconscious flow of the spirit tends by way of consciousness—that is, through the possibility of freedom—to reconnect with the current of light of the blood.

By failing to realize the spirit's autonomy within thinking, we cannot encounter the spirit's light in the blood. This light would jolt us. We are not yet able to draw from the source of the heart. Instead, we are taken hold of by the life of the nervous system, namely by this system's sanguine element. This "being taken hold of" is the alteration of the "I" forces in the blood, where it tends to re-enliven animality, which in ancient times, the spirit could expel from the human form, so that this form could become the vehicle of the "I."

Animality has always been outside the spirit. Today, through the deviated forces of the "I," it becomes internal. It tends to rise again in the form of a mental impulse, as could never happen in human beings. But this is the prelude to the formation of a human-animal race, whose evolution is only vital (etheric)-physical.

Inner chaos and a mechanical system are strictly correlated—one feeds the other.

We humans rejoice, suffer, yearn, anguish, and are exalted, continuously overwhelmed by what can make sense only insofar as it is experienced by us. We do not live in the intact spirituality that still flows through the nervous system, so that it is possible for us to think.

We do not know how we think, and even less do we know the organ by means of which we think. And yet, with this insufficient thinking, we place ourselves before the nervous system, and at the physiological and psychological level, we presume to interpret its function, seeing it in relation to what we cannot perceive except by means of the function we presume to investigate. We seek consciousness not in what manifests as consciousness, but in organs whose vital function is the exclusion of consciousness—organs that exclude it, so that, in reacting to this exclusion, it manifests as waking consciousness, that perceives and thinks.

Therefore no physiology or psychology penetrates the mystery of illness, of anguish, of pain, of longing or of fear: because it is, in any case, an investigation that is itself subjected to the conditions that render illness, anguish, pain, longing and fear, necessary.

In truth, the lance that injures Amfortas is still embedded in the wound. The wound bleeds all the time and no hand can stop it from bleeding, except the hand that knows how to grasp the magic weapon and make of what wounds and kills, that which heals and resurrects.

***

Thought arises therefore as a movement of the spirit, but reflected, thanks to the opposition of corporeality, there, where corporeality, as a nerve substance, is an accomplished process of the spirit, which no longer vitally engages the spirit; it does not hold it back. By means of this (process), therefore, this spirit can flow, not as a formative force but, freely, as a creative virtue.

So that this virtue can give itself conscious form, the minerality of the nerve substance must reflect it. It is the minerality that cannot oppose the flow of the spirit, but at the same time it has the ability to contradict it, allowing the conceiving power to give itself a conscious—therefore, reflected—form, as the inversion of what it is spiritually.

The inversion becomes the vehicle of cosmic forces opposed to the human being.

We can say that the nerve substance is an original bodily system, which has annihilated itself—and this is one of the signs of humanity's Fall—in order to open the gateway to the conscious spirit in earthly corporeality. But so that this system can subsist within the bodily organism, despite its privation of life, it requires the cooperation of processes in which life continues to manifest. Here, still present are the forces that operated during the Fall. Nonetheless, they now become directly operational in the human individuality, because of its more intimate adherence to the nervous system.

The nerve substance is what allows the spirit to flow. This free flow, to know about itself, must have itself reflected. As such, it loses its own inner life. Its free being is abstract. The spirit initially cannot enter the earthly (realm), except as a reflection. Consciousness is in fact reflected.

The Obstructer can now act directly against human beings, because this Obstructor can use the illusory freedom of reflected consciousness, from which flows present-day culture. Now, the Obstructer can use the power of human individuality, operating through the extroversion of the "I." The extroversion is always the reflection.

The extroversion should have been temporary.

The reflection is really abstract thought, which tends to operate as if it were finished thought. In doing so, it is the impediment to the fulfillment of spirit's movement by means of cerebralism.

The free flow of the spirit is compromised. Arrested at reflectivity, it cannot experience the space open to its flow, namely freedom as a real occurrence. Cerebralism that moves thought becomes the reality adverse to the spirit.

Reflectivity, arisen out of the spirit, becomes the field of dialectics opposed to the spirit. The void open by abstract thought is filled by nature.

We humans each mistake nature for our inner self. The whole world of instincts, intellectually legitimized, penetrates into culture, subordinates life to itself, possesses the soul and makes such possession the norm.

The epoch of the maximum individual possibility becomes the epoch of the maximum instinctive expression, through the inversion of the force occurring within the unconscious substratum of abstract thought.

The consciousness soul, corrupting itself in the dialectical artifice, gives rise to the most refined egoism, namely the one of which neither logical nor psychological analysis is possible—psychology and logic, analytical psychology and the most recent speculation, being mere dialectics, that allude to the contents that they possess only as names.

***

The void, in truth, cannot be experienced except through the will. Only willing and thinking can open up the void to the powers of the spirit.

The spirit, in fact, is ordinarily conditioned by the vital opposition of the support, namely by that which enlivens the nerve substance, whose presence is not a direct action as in the remaining corporeality but, rather, reflection—thought.

In the system of the head, the spirit flows through the mineral element, of which it, as a skeletal-nerve organism, can be seen as the initial formative process. In effect, the head tends toward minerality, more than any other bodily region. For this reason, thinking can manifest.

We are not conscious of the spirit's flow. We are in a state of sleep with respect to it. We cannot be aware of such a flow, because it has the power of life. It can become conscious to us only by ceasing to be life, that is, by being reflected by cerebral minerality. In such reflection it is deprived of its own life, in order to emerge as thought.

What is constitutionally mineral in the body allows the spirit to flow intact. This flow is not thinking but, rather, what is reflected as thought. This flow is the true thinking, which we are still incapable of thinking, because we use it to have thoughts, not to actualize it.

The vital processes, instead, are those that, by incarnating the spirit, do not allow it to flow. They compel it to the laws that sustain earthliness—the irreversible thought, already thought. All thinking is instead the possibility of truth, only insofar as it is reversible. The "already-thought" is non-truth, to the extent that it is assumed to be real as the already-thought.

What is simply physical—being the irreversible "already-thought" fixed in its death—cannot oppose the spirit because from the spirit's point of view it is a void. It is the void through which the spirit passes freely. But, for the purposes of consciousness, the spirit can only have the reflection of this, free flowing or passing.

The reflection, as such, is devoid of life. In the reflection, freedom is virtual. Only willful determination can make it actual.

In the vital processes, the mineral element is permeated and moved by the spirit. In the nerve substance, minerality leaves the spirit free. But we do not realize this freedom. To become a fact of consciousness, it must give itself as reflection; it must deprive itself of its own element of life. It is inevitable that being free for us begins as an abstract event—open equally to the lower world as to what dominates and resolves it.

In reflected thought lies the possibility of freedom, but thus, simultaneously, the impediment to it. The impediment is overcome by the thinking that feels the necessity of its own reality. It does not abandon the being from which it arises, but within it, with consciousness actualized as reflected thought, it rediscovers its own sacredness. This makes it necessary to the timelessness of the earth: being, like thought, reversible.

***

In the median seat (heart) and in the limbs, the spirit operates as life, because it is continuously in movement, in order to manifest. In the head the manifestation is complete. For this reason, the spirit itself can manifest, through the system of the head.

But first, as we have seen, only due to a deprivation of life can the spirit express itself as consciousness. This deprivation—becoming the support and determination of a typical inner fact, the individual formation of consciousness—is translated into opposition to the spirit. But the opposition is temporary; it cannot be a permanent condition, as seems to be the inclination of the present-day civilization.

If consciousness, as an egoic fact, is drawn from a negation of life, our task as human beings is to rebuild life through the forces of consciousness which are immediate to us.

An aspect of the flow of extra-terrestrial forces supporting corporeal life manifests as a movement of the limbs.

The human limbs are a symbol of the spirit that operates as the will in space. Their outer figuration is not true except in relation to an incorporeal reality that barely surfaces in the form of movement—an ideal form, if we well observe. No one actually sees the movement but, rather, what it continuously moves.

What manifests as life in the movement of the limbs is just a symbolic sign of the direct emanation of such forces. Meanwhile, in the head, these forces, having edified the nervous system to a point of a completeness that renders it objectively extraneous to them, can flow freely. By reflecting their movement in cerebral physicality, they can become thought (itself).

Since the reflection is the inversion of the movement, it is inevitable that human thought operates as opposed to the spirit.

We can know these forces not in their opposition but, rather, as currents of life in which their principle is revealed, if we experience the process by which we think. But for this (to happen), we need to possess this process. To possess it means to retrace it backwards, all the way to its source.

The exasperated logicism of today, the reactions to traditional philosophizing and the various forms of exaltation of the irrational can be recognized as obscure attempts at autonomy with respect to the thinking process. It has to do with attitudes unaware of that to which they really tend, because they are inevitably closed within the dialectical limit that they presume to identify or overcome. In effect, we need to know thought as a projection of our exclusion from reality, so that we can rediscover reality by means of the redeemed force of thought.

The positivity of thought is its possibility to be recognized as that which is to be retraced. Its positivity is its being able to be re-ascended. But re-ascending its being is not an outer backward repetition of its movement. This would be a further projection of itself into reflectivity, in a different form.

Thought is not a thing, but movement. To retrace its inverse being is the very motion of thought, in its turning no longer toward objects, but toward no object, therefore to itself. Now it relies not on its cerebral support, but on itself. This "relying" on itself leaves the corporeal support free, which thus actualizes its real nature, its pure physicality, to which the spirit is immediate—as a foundation.

The cerebral organ is the irreversible already thought, which in its physicality stands like a gateway open to the spirit, but also like a barrier—an impassable threshold.

5.

THE LIBERATED MENTAL SPHERE

The nervous system is the human primordial corporeality, deprived of primordial light. It is the original physical being shaped by the spirit and later obliged to renounce its own celestial nature, in order to participate in the bodily experience of human beings fallen into minerality.

Inasmuch as it is devoid of its own celestial substance, it no longer bears within itself that for which it was alive before time was born. It is therefore in a state of death, life being for it only identity with its own original light. Meanwhile, the vital experience of the human being has been limited to the demand of animal functions. We live because we exist, not because we think. From animal nature, the nervous system nowadays draws its capacity to exist: an existing that can no longer be its metaphysical light, since it flows to us from a circulatory system that drew its own possibility of life from the degradation of the light, or from the usurpation at the hands of the Obstructers.

The nervous system can be seen as the corpse of the original instrument of the spirit, the celestial organism by means of which primordial humans received the forces, rhythms and harmonies of the stellar world, before plunging into earthly experience proper and elaborating their own mineral structure. For such a structure to arise according to the earthly necessity of the spirit, the original light was taken away from the nervous system and, in the vehicle of the blood, joined with lifeless minerality. It gradually went losing its "stellar" quality and animating the physical form of a fictitious existence, which is the one for which we must be born and die.

Pitted against the nervous system's state of death was the fictitious life of the blood, of which, continuously, in the sacrificial and expiatory rites, the adepts would have to experience reality as a form of death, so that the vision of what (as life) is an emanation of a real and eternal principle could awaken in them. In like manner, the blood shed on the earth, freeing itself of the dead mineral element, could be re-consecrated to the spirit by ritualistic and mystical virtue.

***

In elaborating his terrestrial sheath, the human being had to gradually eliminate what arose as an inferior structure that drew the animal form from the light falling into physicality and from the gradual dis-animation of the nervous system.

The demon of the earth could act within humans through the nerve structure that was abandoned by the light of life, this light having fallen into the physical processes of the blood, from which arose (alongside the mineralization of the physical being) the possibility that humans suffered the impure fire of instincts and passions arising from the blood, namely the power of the fallen light.

Humans could exclusively refer to the transcendent integrity of such power, if, through spiritual practice and ritual, they could awaken the "memory of the blood" and in this sense, feel deeply connected to the principle that transcended their individuality—the spirit of race. The right adherence to their own race protected them. But the further degradation of the light within the blood and the subsequent differentiation of it in the various blood (streams), was to prepare for the era of individuality.

Through the opposition of blood to blood, race to race, the demon of the earth penetrated ever more deeply—as the bearer of sensory darkness—into the decadent nervous system, which, gradually losing the last resonance of the light, could exist at a given moment, only in dead form, as *the god killed within the human being*, buried in the tomb of earthly corporeality.

In the first animal species, the human being's original being went expelling the bodily-soul forms that, along the dis-animation process of the nervous system, did not respond to the sense of their earthly task. Simultaneously, from the same original principle this organism was elaborated for a long time until it became the structure capable of humanly manifesting that of the spirit which is the lowest mode of adherence to earthliness—namely, thought.

Once human beings incarnated, races arose through differentiations of the blood—races, whose form did not correspond to the earthly function of the nervous system and, yet, did not involve the possibility that the soul would open to the "I"-principle. Thus, certain races came to a premature halt on their journey and later regressed. Whereas several others, at a late stage of civilization's development, became immobilized in their original wisdom—typical of Far Eastern races—remaining for millennia identical in that static but increasingly arid splendor, until in new times Westerns, who had had the strength to deprive themselves of the original wisdom's supports in order to conquer the individual form of the "I," were able bring to them the possibility of connecting (by means of the reintegrated forces of the "I") with the basic sense of the human journey—that static and arid splendor finally having to be exhausted.

This time has come; that splendor is indeed exhausted, but the human "I" cannot be said to be born if not in the form that contradicts its spiritual mission. Materialism has compromised human evolution and has paralyzed the possibility of understanding between people, between cultures, between the new and the old, between East and West, the world over.

***

The nervous system is the physical organism that does not belong to the physical sphere. Though sustained, like every entity by the spirit, it is abandoned by the *life* from which it draws origin. Built to manifest a cosmic order of forces, the nervous system has gradually been deprived of its own living cosmic element: in this (lies) the origin of its physical structure and of its projection of animal forms through the evolutionary process. Yet, we humans are but (in a part of our souls) the projection of the fall of the nervous system, and we have the animal category as an external *posterius*—the product of an internal power of discriminative formation.

Nevertheless, today, humans who live solely based on sensory perception, solely in accordance with the life of the senses and therefore with the life of the nerves, risk having animality arise from themselves and of identifying with it.

We tend to bring forth in ourselves the animal that we have never been, if we believe that the brain thinks and that our physical being is evolved matter—as everyone today feels, even if these are capable of thinking differently in the abstract.

Through the nervous system, we experience, in sensations and mental pictures, the world's minerality: because of the most physical substance that in the bodily organism can mediate the spirit. In truth, the mineral element has its own spirit-dependent process in the nervous system, but it cannot be grasped by physiological investigation. What can be grasped by such an investigation does not regard the rising of consciousness.

Through the lifeless nervous system, the spirit, operating as the soul, encounters what is lifeless; it touches minerality. The spirit passes through a vehicle that cannot oppose it, because it is spiritually depleted. But the spirit does not operate directly. It operates by means of the soul. The cerebral organ opposes this soul, functioning as a reflective screen, or as a support, to give rise to consciousness, that is, merely as a mineral intermediary.

Only life can exclude the spirit as a bearer of consciousness, only that which in the nerve system expresses vital processes. The mystery of the soul's life, which is the greatest earthly mystery, is its spiritual form being drawn as an ever-new event from its relationship with the human structure, under the sign of the "I," and in absolute independence from those vital processes. Dependence is the non-reality of the *ego*.

What modern psychologists call the "unconscious" is precisely the psychic area of these vital processes, to the degree in which, by expressing a given nature, they can project themselves through cerebralism in moods and images, which are not thought about, or controlled, but only undergone. In reality, such processes do not have a relationship with the thinking movement, except the one for which, by going beyond their function—as normally happens—they can use its form. From this we see how the substance of the problems resulting from psychology should be traced back to the problem of thought's autonomy.

The cerebral organ's opposition to the spirit, so that thought may arise, is a physical fact, but not perceivable in its function by physiological means, nor psychological ones. Nevertheless, it is a phenomenon that can be called mechanical. At that level, in fact, we begin to be conscious only thanks to a collision with the physical world. We undergo trauma on behalf of that which, devoid of life, makes only what is lifeless appear real to us. Actually, in a certain respect, what is devoid of life within us is only the nervous system, which transmits to us the appearance of the world responsive to its state of dis-animation.

In that way, we ordinarily become victims of a hallucination that we call reality and that draws its possibility of being from our inner life that is denied in its illusory vision. Essentially, only structural forces are real, but they are imperceptible to the senses. At that level, we can only produce what is dead—namely, the machine, rationalistic culture. But we produce them by negating the life in which flows a force that is our own and that we can know.

The brain's purely physiological processes have nothing to do with thinking, just as a utensil has no other relationship with whoever uses it, except that of responding to the external use required, and not because such a use activates inner functions. Undoubtedly, for what is asked of it, it is important that the utensil be efficient.

The organic opposition of the cerebral system to the spirit's motion, as a function imperceptible to the senses, cannot be physically, or psycho-physiologically investigated, except in the aspect of its alterity, or of its non-relation—namely, as a mechanical movement objectively extraneous to the life of thinking, which flows from another direction.

***

The positivity of the nervous system is its minerality, that is, its not being an impediment to the spirit. Through the nervous substance, the spirit touches the physical world.

For the spirit, the mineral is the void, namely that which cannot pose an obstacle to it: that which does not hold back the flow of the spirit. But outwardly, it *appears* to reflected consciousness as if it were full—the opposite being true. Fullness is there to be realized as an inner weft, not to be consecrated as it appears. Each time such reality is actualized, which is an emptying of the form's density. But it is not perceived.

In this lies the secret of our current experience. Wherever we see minerality elaborated as the form of beings and of things, we should not renounce recognizing form as a purely ideal value, which rises up visible not through the spirit, but through its reflection. The form is always an internal relation, that is, an edifying motion where we gather our inner life on the verge of rising again from reflectivity. Matter is really the void. But in order for consciousness to realize this void, it must draw it from its own reflexivity as from the experience of a "fullness"—the fullness, redeemed by reflexivity, being the void, which we always experience, unknowingly. And we do not know it because we would not be able to bear it.

Precisely in what, as void, the system of nerves is worth to the spirit, this surfaces as individual consciousness. But (it does not surface) as an awareness of the void, rather, as a "product" of its arising from the void. Not as the awareness of non-corporeality, not as the awareness of the void that renders it possible—such awareness still having to blossom.

Consciousness is the embryonic mode of being of the "I"; it is not the "I."

The calmness of the cerebral organ is essentially its ontological reality. It is the initial possibility of actualizing the void that already is: from which thought arises; however, without such thought actually knowing its own origin.

Spiritual practitioners of the new times work in this direction.

***

The autonomy of thinking leaves the cerebral organ free, which thus achieves its constitutional rest, the positive being of its death: which is an organic reality, already completed.

In the cerebral organ's stillness, thought can experience the "void" as a structural reality of the nervous system. This is its conversion. It is the void that thought can achieve as it identifies with its own movement, drawing (by means of it) upon the virtue from which it emanates, without which it would not be able to arise as thought.

In rational thought, in abstract thought, we have, in negative form, the possibility of the void. Ancient ascetics had to avoid the dialectical experience of thinking to attain the void. They had to cancel thinking. Modern experimenters must possess thinking, namely *enter into the negativity of its movement.*

All humans, who truly are of this time, have the possibility of the void, in the fact that we think. Our task as spiritual practitioners is simple; we must gather the flow of the spirit through the dis-animated nervous system—but within thinking, not within the object of thinking, not within dialectics.

This task is extremely simple. For this reason, it is difficult to understand, because we believe we have thinking, but we have only its reflection.

To the extent that the cerebral system needs the vital forces to subsist in the bodily organism, it draws them from a corporal-instinctive life that tends to express itself by means of thought. This is dialectics. Nor does corporeal nature express itself through cerebralism by what can objectively be of value to the spirit, but by what of an irregular invisible world—operating on the adaptations of its structure to the earthly necessity of consciousness—tends by means of it to determine the soul. Indebted to such an irregular relationship are the psyche's various pathological phenomena—intellectualism, scientism, dialectics and mediumship. The soul grasped by corporeality transforms the spirit's forces into destructive currents through corporeality.

In reality, the experience of the senses, which is arrested at the sensory (level) and remains obtuse regarding what the perceptions bear of the supra-sensory in sensory guise, prepares the methodical madness of human beings, insofar as they continuously place it against the inner reality that penetrates the soul, unnoticed, by means of perceptions. In truth, it penetrates unrecognized, unaccepted, in that, we, conditioned by cerebralism, unknowingly arrest it at the threshold of consciousness. But we receive it in the depths, and in waking life we work against it.

Only independence from the cerebral organ gives us a way to knowingly receive the inner life of which perceptions are the vehicle. We will have to discover that perceptions are a means, not an end.

A deformation of all existence derives from the fact that we mistake perceptions themselves for the object of perceiving. In that way, the whole world of facts becomes true and overwhelming. It modifies human life, being instead the vehicle through which life tends to reveal itself to us.

In ordinary perceiving, the experience of the world is continuously lost, insofar as it is reduced to mental image and sensation, without hope that life imagined in the organic world, in plants and in animated beings, can become perception, just as its immediate appearance is perception.

Appearance is already the beginning of our communion with such a life, immediately suppressed by the egoic necessity of consciousness.

In reality, human culture today has nothing to do with that for which we are on earth. It actually contradicts it.

For this reason, we cannot know calmness. We mistake inertia or the cessation of agitation for calmness. We lack the inner measure for what is calmness. We continuously oppose the soul's secret communion with the world. We do not know the soul, but only its alteration.

***

Calmness is not an internal state among others. It is not a mood that opposes others, but the dimension proper to the soul's being, which is experienced as such only in rare moments.

Non-tranquility, namely agitation, is the soul that is not implemented, the soul impeded from being what it is in its true essence, by the resonance of the nervous system's alterations within it, since this system, psychophysically, goes beyond its natural mediation.

In its function regarding the life of the senses, the nervous system is an instrument that, used unilaterally and irregularly, cannot but deteriorate.

The alteration of the nerve apparatus is becoming normality. Today, human beings, consciously calm, may appear abnormal. Or mistaken for calm individuals are those who are powerless to feel.

The structure of the nervous system is such that on the one hand it sinks into physical corporeality, and on the other it borders on the incorporeal. Its equilibrium lies in the possibility for the sensory element to be counterbalanced by a correlative inner activity. If this does not occur, the organ deteriorates.

From a strictly biological point of view, the human brain is in a descending phase of its evolution. An involution is taking place whose reasons escape scientific investigation and that therefore only an objective act of consciousness, independent of the physical course of such an organ, could know and value. If it is true that thought is not born from the brain, but expresses itself by means of it, it is obvious that within the original forces of thought lies the possibility of an action independent of its organ.

Such an action is possible because it is logically congenial to the sense of the human structure. In fact, only in the human being can freedom be realized.

The nervous system should mediate the sensory experience to the spirit. It should be the spirit's instrument in the sensory (realm). But the instrument is altered through its irregular use by consciousness. Sense experience overwhelms the spirit, penetrating into the individual interiority more than can be processed by it. The nerve vehicle is not retraced by the inner current that the sensory content stimulates.

***

The experience of the senses overwhelms the spirit; it comes to use the spirit. One can say that it is not the spirit that carries out the experience of the senses, rather the spirit dominated by this (experience), but unaware; and so the thing, the phenomenon, nature are valuable in being impenetrable to the spirit, which nevertheless assumes them as penetrated. It is the inversion that we say it should be reversed, according to a movement that is always less possible to the weakened but albeit strictly contemporary dialectical thought.

It is the inversion that nevertheless occurs together with a process of the nervous system's alteration, to which are connected series of physical ailments incurable by a therapy incapable of grasping the true causes.

The breakdown of the nervous system reverberates in turn in the unhealthy life of consciousness, which can hardly be identified by medicine or by psychology, themselves produced by the mental (realm) to which the breakdown is traced back.

Forces of the spirit, grasped and altered by the sensory (realm), come to be valued in the various forms of culture. They come to be valued not only scientifically, but ethically and religiously. Unaware of their profound abdication, they seek a compensation even in the form of traditional orthodoxy.

Sensory experience, devoid of an inner counterpart, cannot but alter the vehicle by means of which it is fulfilled, since this vehicle has been physiologically formed by the original spiritual forces through the manifestation of the subject of the experience. The subject is excluded from the "matter" of its own experience. *It is an impossible contradiction, in that the subject can never really be excluded.* The experience is carried out according to the inversion of the force set into motion for its fulfillment. What is thus carried out is something whose destructive power projected in time is not imagined.

The breakdown of the nervous system is therefore reflected in the soul. It is the gradual path to neurosis, to hysteria, that is, to longing and to fear—to immorality scientifically justified.

In reality, the cerebral individual is a being through which the forces that have the task of destroying the life of the soul can methodically organize themselves—the spirit's direct instrument being the soul, not the body.

Such human beings can no longer know calmness. They can only know a form of precarious detachment, an obtuse and fragile self-isolation, (both) continuously destined to reveal their inconsistency.

The spirit needs to be grasped in the pure interiority through soul forces; for us as investigators, it does not have to flow directly into corporeality. We cannot encounter it in the sensory organism, where its force, devoid of animic (soul) mediation, burns the physical being, changes or is inverted. The breakdown of the nervous system becomes the path for the demolition of the human being's physio-psychic equilibrium.

The spirit, not encountered by the investigator through the highest and most volitional consciousness, descends directly into corporeality by way of an unconscious path, or by means of exercises that solicit its sensory manifestation. In this way, it operates as a destructive force for the health of the body and of the soul.

Each sensory manifestation of the inner experience, which is not the consequence of the human being's conscious encounter with the incorporeal forces of the spirit, does not come from the supra-sensory, but from its alteration. It is really spiritualism, behind which urge cosmic powers adverse to the human being.

**

To achieve the stillness and isolation of the cerebral system means to notice the point of thought's dependence on the breath and to work toward freeing thought from such dependence: from which, by way of thought, feeling and willing are imprinted.

Thought freed from the unconscious dependence on the breath realizes the flow of the light, once required for *pranayama*.

Any practice of yogic breathing today acts in the opposite direction to possible independence. By means of the alternate rise of the cerebrospinal liquid, controlled breathing operates on the brain, stimulating its sanguine (blood) and metabolic element, that is, an order of processes functionally opposed to those to which the highest manifestations of consciousness are connected. In fact, it has the task of nourishing the life that the cerebral system demands to the strictest extent necessary for sensory and thinking mediation.

These are vital processes graspable by physiological investigation, but therefore unidentifiable with what occurs in the cerebral organ when thought emerges. What occurs in the brain as a result of thought escapes the purely physical investigation. It can be perceived only through the forces that manifest in the thinking activity. But, for this reason, thought must be penetrated.

No vital process actually produces thought, concerning only the connection of the cerebral system with the remaining organism. Nonetheless, life processes can act upon thought as extraneous processes, capable of assuming the form of personal thought. Then it is nature that thinks, not thought: thought having little self-awareness. It is the condition of ordinary human beings.

On the other hand, nature, race, destiny in its less conscious and therefore more constrictive aspect have no other vehicle to control the human being.

The more the cerebral organ physiologically responds to the function for which it was formed, and yet escapes the prevalence of the sanguine-metabolic element, subordinating it to its own mobility, that is, to the need of mediating thought, the more we as humans are independent of a bodily consciousness through which the instinctive being infiltrates. This instinctive being in reality infiltrates in order to be known gradually, as the bearer of the profound forces of the "I," which ask to be reconnected with the "I."

The spurious knowledge of oneself, rather than be surpassed, is reinforced and exalted by means of breathing exercises, in which the breath is illusorily controlled by thought that does not know how to gather the subconscious connection to the respiratory function. This reaffirms the power that it has over thought, as a power of the human being's Obstructers. It is the path to the exaltation of instinctivity and animality—opposite to the spirit.

In reality, forces that ordinarily tend to express themselves in the form of thought act by means of the brain's vital and rhythmic processes, necessary in themselves, due to the fact that through human thought they can conquer another dimension of their own being. They grasp the soul and the human possibility of freedom, with the aim of eliminating them, using them for purposes that we—illusorily free—mistake for our own.

The area where thought manifests is in fact the only one where the spirit can break through by eliminating life processes.

When these processes develop an activity higher than that required by the vital economy of the brain, in function of thought, they obstruct the autonomy of thinking, which is the only supra-sensory possibility of modern human beings. Thinking should in fact acquire such autonomy and vitality, so as to become independent of the structural necessity of the organ.

The act of thinking is free insofar as it takes place apart from any relationship with the life forces of the brain and it allows these (life forces) to operate according to their law, in a rhythmic and metabolic sense. No thinking is free as a mere act but, rather, insofar as it, as an act, is experienced volitionally or meditatively outside of the cerebral determinism, that contains its law and is therefore able to dominate it.

One thing is the autonomy of the life forces that spiritual practitioners can give to their own corporeal being through thought's disengagement from cerebralism, another is the autonomy that such forces have insofar as they express a given nature; a given nature being the totality of the life forces operating according to the animal condition necessary for the bodily expression of the ego.

***

That which is called destiny is a current of forces that, in order to reach us from the depths of the soul, passes through the bodily nature and through the outer world, since we lack the sufficient power of consciousness to receive it directly into ourselves. It is the reason for the elusiveness or impenetrability of destiny, and therefore of the negative forms that it must assume in its passage through corporeality and sensory exteriority. Meanwhile, as a creative power, it can be known and encountered there, where it emerges as a fundamental will of the inner human being.

The secret of the inner human being is to prevent the spirit's forces from passing directly to corporeality or being mediated for us by physical events.

An adverse destiny does not exist. It is adverse only because of the *maya* by which the soul is taken. In reality, the soul is the non-conscious bearer of *karma*. The "I" lies outside the necessity of *karma*, being its pre-natal preparer. On earth, it can only be its experiencer. The art is precisely to be the "I"; the "I" and the inner human being must coincide. The soul becomes conscious of *karma* there, where it encounters the "I," or is encountered by it.

From that point in which we come to say "I" to ourselves, we can contemplate our own destiny, insofar as we are one with the eternal element passing from life to life. We can contemplate the soul, or its radical forces. Only in this way can we discover what no intelligence can give us. In those moments, we are not supported by the soul but, rather, by the "I" itself in its transcendence.

The transcendence is truly immanent. The relationship between the contingent "I" and the higher "I" is not graspable with any human logic, but only within the inner movement that realizes it, which is the profound presence of the Logos in us. The identity of our free being.

***

We do not dream of the ancient; we do not dream of the new. We must start from what is now. We must operate within the forces by means of which we already begin to know.

Today the spirit is no longer—like in ancient times—blood or race. It is no longer nature. Rather, it is what, living within the depths of nature, arises as a conscious principle, on the condition on disentangling itself from it, of continuously extinguishing it to express itself—without yet truly doing so, for this self-expression would be achieved in recreating it.

The spirit is no longer spontaneity, but primarily will. And not immediate will, but that which can be realized consciously, according to the immediate process of willing. Only such a will can restore the spontaneity and the power of impersonality.

But the will is the force that does not allow itself to be grasped by egoic consciousness. It cannot allow itself to be grasped because ordinarily it wills insofar as it is the one that grasps instinctively. The will not willed by the "I" is nature. *The most tenacious force of the ego is precisely its passive dependence on such a will.*

In pure thought, freed of dialectical debris, the spontaneous will that normally manifests as the limbs' motor force and as the creative process of perceiving, can be willed. Likewise, this magical will can be gathered directly in the movement of the limbs and in perceiving, but on condition that it has already been encountered as the "life of light" of thinking.

***

Nature rules in the ordinary breath. In modern times, no controlled breath can grasp nature, because the breath expresses nature. We breathe to be alive. In essence, in the presumed respiratory spiritual practice of modern *yogis,* one begins from a subjection to nature and presumes to utilize this subjection to move beyond nature, without realizing that this would have the opposite effect.

We would need to begin with the only activity that arises from an opposition to nature—thinking. But thinking according to the experience that it itself demands with its immediate movement, not the thinking that, unaware of itself, submits to (something) "already-thought," devoid of connection with the reality of the present-day soul.

No breathing practice today can revive the ancient *yoga*, just like no meditative practice that presumes to be *yoga*, unless it leads to the modern spiritual practice of thinking, which does not require breathing practices to become real. On the contrary, it is possible only on condition of freeing itself from the support of the breath. It is the spiritual practice that enables the breath to realize its autonomy from the nervous system, namely an agreement that it originally had with such a system.

The breath's original autonomy is a metaphysical movement of the breath, which is not a breathing, but an assimilating of the light, beyond the necessity of the breath. It is the nourishment of light that operates in the secret of life, as an inverted breath, that excludes the ordinary breath. It separates from it. It has no need of it. It ignores it, to the point of not impeding its extinction. It is the magical path of the coming times.

***

The intervention of the intellectual will, or of ordinary "mental picturing" bound to the sensory (realm), paralyzes the possibility for the breath to leave the light's movement free. It binds the soul to the animal breath, which is the "subtle" condition of selfishness.

We are normally bound to cerebralism with the ordinary breath. This bond is strengthened through the spurious breathing practice. But then we have to admit the consequences of the fact that the process is reversible. Each mood, occurring through a normal psychosomatic identification with the breath cannot but reverberate in cerebralism, and consequently affect the mental (sphere), forcing it to reactions that do not belong to the free human being.

Today, those who practice *pranayama*, are more subtly bound to the system of the head. They willfully exclude the spirit. They make it impossible to distinguish "free imagining" from the imagining that is arbitrary, since they do not know, nor are they able, to untie imagination from physiological processes. They believe imagination to be that to which it is bound. By unconsciously identifying with cerebralism, they are even more subjected than usual to the pressure of instincts and of emotions, through the cerebral system, which is the place by means of which they can assert themselves.

Those who really follow the path of knowledge, nor illusorily aspire to find again the forces of life, know they must loosen intelligence from the system of the head, so that intelligence and consciousness can coincide.

Each mental concentration that does not involve the independence of consciousness from the instinctive being inherent in cerebral physicality, binds consciousness ever more to corporeality and operates against the spirit.

In so doing, they achieve a result opposite to that achieved by the ancient *yogi*, who, by means of *pranayama,* tended toward a communion with the profound forces of feeling and of willing, in order to achieve independence from the mental (sphere).

The practice that once freed ascetics from the mental (sphere) and connected them with the forces that edify corporeality, today binds them to corporeality, since they lack the supra-sensory mediation proper to the nature of ancient human beings. It is a technique relative to a given constitution and to a given animalistic form, that is to say, relative to that of the human being, which, in the inner order, has the character of mutability; form and constitution being what, as a vestment of the original, enters into time and becomes.

This technique, taken up again by modern human beings, is reduced to an abstract mechanism, valid at most as a physical exercise, insofar as it appeals to a breath of which it has only the sensory movement, without being able to act on the inner counterpart, since it does not perceive it. Each internalization of such breathing, performed by modern humans, does not overcome its abstract physicality but reinforces it, because it psychically energizes the mental-cerebral bond, which we are unable to see. The mental (sphere) that would release itself from such a constraint would not need *pranayama,* because it would have within itself what it asks of it.

***

It is a mistake to believe that the "non-mental" is the spiritual, or the threshold to the spiritual. There is a long area where the spiritual is the mental, for which the task should truly be the extinction of what we believe to be spiritual. But only that with which we are not identified can be extinguished.

Rather, we should say that the "non-mental." is the beginning of the true mental being. The spirit cannot but express itself in it. The spirit that operates in the soul is the pure mental (being), liberated thought, the principle of the dis-identification.

The mind must be there, as the essence or the conscious unity of thinking, feeling and willing.

To exist, it needs to not be what it is not.

To not be what it is not, it must know how, continuously, it is what it is not, in believing itself to be. The penetration of its own being to free itself of its illusory being, is the secret of thought.

The secret of thought is the secret thinking. It is the thinking that escapes thoughts, namely the thinking that can be thought because it does not express itself. We think without thinking it. Therefore, it is not extinguished. It is alive. And it is the subtle sense of the world.

In the thinking that does not think, the mental (being) is gathered and becomes empty of what it is not.

Thought begins to truly think the reality of the world when it ceases to think, so that it and the reality of the world are one.

The true experience of the senses is possible for this thought that does not dissolve into sensations, but is strengthened by being alive in them.

Mental silence is the birth of the thinking that is one with the world's entities. Therefore, it is the first mode of being of the mental, based on the freeing of human and worldly ties. Through its essential independence, it can penetrate the sensory realm.

The mind begins to be true in contrast to what it is not. In knowing what it is not, it knows how to extinguish this knowing, because the projected movement within it, no longer having a personal form, is used by the reality of the world; it manifests itself through it.

The pure movement used by the world's true being is the very spirit of the world that manifests within the human depths. Such is the sense of the "non-mental."

The realization of the mind is ultimately the affirmation of what it is without knowing it. There would be no thought of what the world is, if there were not already a secret union with the world.

The mind must be the mind, not its support, not its manifestation, not the thought of things.

Thought is always the mental being of the "non-mental," but it is important to be so much in the act of thinking and positively in that act as to notice the light by means of which we truly think—the light that is not outside, but inside of thinking.

Therefore, we cannot think the light.

Those of us who seek the "non-mental," either of yoga or of the Tao, or of Mahayana, bind the mental to new mental projections or esoteric "mentalisms." Meanwhile, we should realize that we are each the mind and that we are not really the mind.

***

Our art as spiritual practitioners is to discover the force we draw upon in the work of liberation—not to look for this force outside the point from which it moves, if we want to grasp the true subject. We can experience this subject as a *transcendent,* which rests within, because we are this (true subject), even if we fail to notice it. The will that we put into action must not lead us to anything other than that from which we move, on this side of a subjective limit whose subject we must identify.

The subject has no other identity than with itself. But this identity with itself lies beyond the ego and its highest intellectual forms. It is there, where the ego is no longer anything: this (identity) being its invincible force.

To will in the world, we ordinary humans need objects, otherwise we would not know how to will. In wanting to free ourselves, we begin to will something that is not an object, but simply willing (itself)—the very movement within the vehicle of thought. This will is the invisible fabric of the world, which reveals itself to us, to the extent that we experience it not by means of the ego, but by means of the principle in which the ego annihilates itself.

If we stand before the scene of the world with this will in which thought is gathered, the world in its internal movement begins to arise before us in images of light. The principle of pure light begins to live in us as a subject whose egoic form dies with respect to the sense world.

The constraints of the ego are not sensory perceptions, but the fictitious values to which it gives rise from its immediate identification with them.

***

When the mental (sphere) is so purified that it coincides with the original structure of the physical being, then the spirit is within consciousness; the eye can look at the world. Through the world, it looks at the spirit.

The spirit does not have matter opposed to it. It has no error against itself, but its own becoming truth.

Prior to such a moment, the eye looks without seeing. In reality, it does not look, because there is no *subject* of the looking; there is no "I." We each believe we see, for the fact that we look. In reality, no one looks by immersing the "seeing" into things. Ordinary looking is a continuous escape from the eye that looks. For this reason, it does not have anything that it can see.

When the mental (sphere) descends into such calmness to realize that its own immateriality is not touched by bodily processes, then it coincides with the incorporeal foundation of the head. It begins to experience within itself the original process of physical matter. It actualizes within itself, inverted, the movement from which the spiritual precipitates into minerality.

Minerality becomes the support of the highest inner experience.

When the mental is annihilated, then the mind is the foundation in the human being—the identical foundation of the spirit and of its corporeal organ. Then, the support is left.

The support left behind acquires a new function—new in that it restores the *primordial*; it returns to being what it was when the spirit was life.

Its material non-entity is experienced as the adamantine depths. Its primordial light is recovered.

As a physical organ realized in its material non-entity, the support is released from the animal category. Ceasing to be a mediator, it can function as the *spirit's substance*, as a body of the light, its original substance being the soul of the light.

What has been lost begins to be found. What was taken from us is restored, to the degree in which we are free—and such a degree becomes life itself, the human relation.

What was lost is restored, because the light of thinking is the Logos—the light that can be found again because it again flows in the world. Every day it flows in ordinary thinking, unknown.

It began to flow again in the human soul in the most unrecognizable guise—as rational thought.

The light truly comes from the West.

For it to be recognized, the soul must be educated in the thought of the Hierarchies. What must be recognized is the non-human impersonality of the light bearers, to whose level the personal human element can be brought only by rising to it, by not reducing it to names, to forms, to signs, to relationships provisionally necessary to its own limit.

To the gods, what matters is not the devotional shrewdness necessary for good human conscience, or the diligent exposition of spiritualistic theory, but the soul's genuine movement with respect to the reality of the cosmos, that the gods support. True meditating joins the human to the Divine and suggests the form of thought, namely true action.

***

What can alter the calm of human beings is always a thought that we do not actually think, because we do not have it as the object of our thinking, but are subjected to: a fact or a mood, that we are incapable of thinking and thus experiencing, (thereby) remaining ourselves. Only if we remain ourselves—that is, free—can we experience something other than ourselves, to the extent that we are able to identify with it, by knowing it—or rather, by willing it.

To identify with things or with forces and *not to be aware of this*, in knowing them, is the error: the error that we are unable to see. But the error must be there, in order for it to be seen one day.

Identification is the act proper to the spirit, which gives rise to error or to truth, according to the "I"'s level of assent, according to the correspondence of its waking state to intimate sleep, where its secret being lies, one with the world, its "more-than-being-awake," capable of deeply penetrating the waking state—the possibility of freely giving ourselves to things in knowing them.

Things, facts, inner and outer needs are what we ordinary humans are incapable of thinking and which yet rise up to us as thought: which we believe we think, but in reality we feed the thought needed to destroy the light and the life of thinking.

No thinking can disturb the person who knows meditation, because meditation is the true thinking. Facts remain facts; things remain things; they do not become thought. But, for this reason, thinking moves in their weft. It penetrates their transcendent exteriority. This thinking is not really mechanical rationality, but a non-dialectical communion, a movement of the soul.

Thought that is neither intuition nor meditation is frivolous, even if it is philosophical.

Any thought bound to human facts or to worldly values, is false, even if it is necessary or rises to cultural dignity. Knowing, insofar as it is an abstract amalgamation of notions—in its systematization that has become extraneous and opposed to the thinking from which it arises and that alone justifies its thinkability—is false.

The thinking necessary for everyday life manifests as the continuous death of thought; therefore we say "I think," but in reality thought is destroyed and we know deep down that it is a lost opportunity. We are said to think what we do not actually think, or is lost insofar as one thinks.

This dying of thought has, within the speculative order, a formal arrangement, which tends to describe it as a process of thought, insofar as we contemplate it closed within judgment and within language, while actually it is the process of the loss of thought. And it is logic.

In logic, thought is grasped, there, where ceasing to be alive, it ceases to be true. From this there arises the philosophical, abstract, mathematical effort to fix as a form of truth something that is valid only insofar as it presupposes it. And it presupposes it already made, so that logic can justify its objectivity, eluding the thinking by which it was made.

Nevertheless, with respect to facts and human interests, logic is not only the true connection, but the necessary one.

Such truth and such necessity become false, when they become a rule for thought. Likewise, it makes no sense for moods or sentiments, which determine the value of life, to be aroused by the logical articulation of facts and human interests that with the soul could have no other relation except their resolution or their rectification, namely their reduction to truth, not their rational legitimization.

Moods and sentiments are rightly aroused only by thought that penetrates the essence of facts and of human interests. But such thought is not logic.

A judgment, or a logical construct, can justly awaken a sentiment, only in relation to its level of truth, or even insofar as it is assumed as a theme of concentration on par with any other theme. But the level of truth of a judgment is not the logical form, which undoubtedly has its function but, rather, that which gives rise to such a form.

Each thought that is not a meditation, is not free; unfree, such thought is not true.

**

It is legitimate to open up to sentiments that respond to the reality of the world, and not to its appearing. Each time a sentiment is aroused by mere appearance, it proves to be deceitful.

Thus, no thought really disturbs the thinking of spiritual practitioners, even if it arises in them as deceitful thought. The deceit is necessary to its possibility of recognition. For them each thought is the truth, because in it, thinking is, in any case, true—as movement.

But this truth, when it can be objective thought, is not only form but also content: of feeling and of willing.

Likewise, the feeling aroused by objective thought becomes thought's force of inspiration, for the fact that feeling connects with its own truth in thinking.

Human discord arises from the fact that instinctive feeling takes advantage of the thought's lack of clarity, for which we judge not according to objective thought, but according to subjective attraction or repulsion, to which the objective virtue of thought is subordinated. For example, we are not able to understand others, because we are incapable of thinking what we objectively should about them, beyond the emergence of immediate sentiments of antipathy, which we are unable to glimpse because they are more intimate than the thinking that expresses them. They act in place of thought, as personal nature. We do not think, but nature thinks and justifies itself logically, or spiritually.

No thought can really disturb the calm of spiritual practitioners, who train themselves to find the pure element of thinking that does not rise up from corporeality—namely, their inner willing. A thought can disturb the calm of spiritual practitioners because they do not close themselves off to it obtusely, nor do they allow themselves to be overwhelmed by it, but they grasp, within the mood, the resonance of feeling, the life of willing. They take from them the secret architecture of thinking.

A disturbing thought is precious to the spiritual practitioner, as the sign of a force that needs to be rediscovered, of a thought purer and higher that cannot be cognized differently.

By analogous movement, suffering is the help of which thought is enlivened, insofar as it frees pain from the element of darkness necessary for the soul's opposition to the light—the inevitable opposition to the ego. The light being the real life of thought.

6.

Spirit and Rhetoric

Within thinking lies feeling; within feeling lies the will; within the will lies the "I." This "I" is to be discovered.

Within ancient humans, thinking was the vestment of the spirit. It could not be intellectualistic in the modern sense, because it did not need to be. Its support was internal, insofar as cerebralism had only a mediating function for the expressive act. When thinking fell into error, this was not due to intellectualism but, rather, to the emergence of the lower nature and, consequently, to the loss of contact with the light of the higher nature, and therefore of the ritual, of the traditional order.

Ancient humans could encounter their own "I" as a higher entity, apart from corporeality. In them, the support of consciousness was incorporeal, not through self-awareness of the inner being but, rather, by way of the structural virtue of consciousness. This virtue was spiritual in its simply natural emergence. For the ascetic, wisdom was to rely on the immediacy of the original purity. Spiritual practice was the exercise of eliminating the individual element.

Initiation acted through a *spiritual nature,* insofar as it could bring spontaneous forces of will to levels of light, namely forces unaltered by sensory experience, or purified by the influences of this (sensory experience) thanks to a specific spiritual practice. Sensory experience was carried out directly by the inner being, not through autonomous forces of the intellect; an internal inspiration—where certain inner norms were observed—revealed the secrets of the physical world to human beings. But humans themselves lacked consciousness of the physical world: a consciousness that in reality we still have to conquer: (that) we should be on the way to conquering, if everything now were not compromised.

The ancient human being's experience of the "I" was incorporeal and grandiose. In modern humans, it has become corporeal and prosaic. In modern humans, the inner being, through the attainment of earthly consciousness, adheres physically to corporeality, but becomes unaware of adhering to it as a supra-sensory being. Falling into reflected mental picturing, we believe we are of the same make as what we experience as sensory. For this reason, we have stopped at the threshold of the physical world. We have not penetrated it, but it has penetrated us, asserting itself with our forces and establishing itself against us as an impenetrable alterity.

"Materialism" is actually what prevents us from penetrating matter, in which we investigate as if in an "objectivity" categorically opposed to us, and now, above all, projected into that "nuclear" alterity, which—in various forms of an abstract nullification, with the correlative myths of "anti-matter," truly dreamed—confirms its impenetrability: the adamantine obtuseness of the subject, which notices everything except him or herself.

It is a difficult fate of the "I," the author of everything and yet forced to remain ignored. Moreover, it is overwhelmed by what it does. It is prohibited from knowing anything about itself. Today, the tendency to know it is seen as an unreal investigation; it is the object of mockery. The most logical assumption is considered absurd.

***

For now, each human being is only theoretically an "I," because we know nothing about the "I" that we each say we are, being actually interested in the body, namely the sensory form of the "I," with which we unknowingly identify. We come to mistake corporeal and instinctive needs for the needs of the "I," and, by organizing our whole lives and even our culture in function of such needs, we presume to work for the "I," that is, for an entity to which we instead reserve only abstract philosophical and psychological discussions.

Human egoism today is not, in fact, true individualism, but simply the love of physical corporeality. If it were authentic individualism, we would already be on the right path, because we would act according to the forces of the "I" independent of the corporeal being. We would dominate corporeality.

The theme of ancient ascetics was to free themselves of the individual element. The theme of spiritual practitioners today is not to lose it but, rather, to implement it.

***

We believe that the forces by means of which we experience the physical world and our own corporeal beings belong to corporeality. We are unable to enter into the secret of the physical world, because we ignore within ourselves the incorporeal forces that penetrate our own corporeality. Our inner being—to the extent that it is reflected in corporeality—assumes the cerebral organ as a temporary support by becoming estranged from its own current of life. But with this, in the positivistic form of thought, it trains itself to an autonomy in the sensory (realm) toward which it indirectly opens the passage to the high forces of the "I." The tragedy is that, despite so much analytical self-consciousness, we fail to become aware of it.

To ignore the descent of these forces into the "materialistic" form, to ignore their supra-sensory nature despite their giving rise to the outer image of the world, is our contradictory situation today.

In reality, thought binds itself to the sensory support in order to develop the force to free itself from it. Only this force in fact can penetrate the depths of the sensory (realm).

Thought that seems the most practical is really the most painfully abstract, because it believes it gathers in scientific or technical or linguistic categories the content of a reality that arises as the reflection of the un-reflected power of consciousness and that from the depths demands to refer to this as the category of categories, or an archetypal category.

Thinking falls into the sensory (realm), but here its constriction to rationality and to self-consciousness develops inner forces, whose peculiar virtue is the possibility to retrace its own process backwards. The possibility of the re-ascension for us begins here.

***

The long night of Kali-Yuga is actually over, but we humans have lost the possibility of knowing it. We no longer know how to distinguish dialectics from thought, the tradition as a past legacy from its content of perpetuity and, therefore, we ignore the virtue of rebirth and the principle's unpredictability of movement of the manifest as well as of the non-manifest. We mistake its ritual and grammatical form for Tradition, thereby falling into the same nominalism to which the intellect gives rise in its various forms of present-day knowing, which seems to express the "I" but excludes it. Meanwhile, the converging in itself should appear to thought (as) the first actualization of the "I" within its own movement and the initial possibility of accessing its own metaphysical value.

Thus, the science of logic, in its claim to constitute itself as a mathematical system for the identification of thought with language, is not only the attempt to mechanize the discourse, but to fix thought in its fall, so that it is impossible for it to retrace its own process backwards. In essence, we consecrate the forms of the fall with the forces that awaken from it for the re-ascension.

Retracing its own process is for thought the crowning of its logic—the ultimate meaning of its temporary separation from the original spiritual form.

Mathematical logic can be useful for a certain type of scientific exposition, but a dialectic of reality cannot become true except with the dynamic pulverization of all logic, for the expression of the unforeseeable element of thinking, namely the element of life, outside of dialectical death, in which alone the sense of everyday reality—the living content of the Tradition—can rise again.

***

The logic that we attempt to fix as a system for the discursive identification of reality—not gathering of this but the transitory, finite and therefore numerable elements—cannot be but the logic of death.

In this death life urges (forth), just as in the mechanical world mental power urges and deteriorates; in abstract society, in abstract politics, in abstract wellbeing, in senseless but organized existence, the power of the spirit urges and destroys itself unknown. We must see how this destruction is perpetuated and how the sense of life is lost more each day, so that the whole force is used for the continuation of an unsustainable situation, since we are no longer able to conceive of a different one: not knowing the force that engages and destroys in such a struggle.

Within thinking is feeling, within feeling is willing, within willing is the "I." Thinking, separated from the internal forces and grasped by the sensory, subordinates the internal forces to its own abstractness and corrupts them—there, where its task would be to draw on such forces to make of its own abstract arbitrariness a concrete power of freedom.

The will is always abstract. Its living power comes from nature, which clothes itself in freedom.

***

Where abstractness subsists without the liberation of thinking, nature expresses itself as the power of life and governs us by means of the mechanism of cerebralism. It is the state of the present-day culture.

By means of the cerebral instrument, nature becomes mentalized*, because thought, estranged from the spirit, identifies its freedom with cerebral logicism—which is its serving of bodily impulses, while considering itself autonomous. Through the head, we regress into animality, because the spirit cannot give anything more through the cerebral organ that subjugates thought to itself, insofar as thought, limited to being abstract, no longer has strength.

Abstractness cannot be an end. Therefore, it cannot put an end to us. It is a means, a process of mental transition, toward what surpasses it, as well as toward what degrades it.

As a process of transition from the corporeal to the spiritual, abstract thought is the possibility of freedom.

However, the moment of the positive possibility of abstract thought is short. For a large part of present-day culture it has already expired.

It is followed by the return of the living element under the sign of both animality and the inner human being.

---

*   mentalize – to make mental in nature and not physical.

Animality and instinctivity translated into value, justified scientifically, converted into a world vision, with a relative religious, spiritualistic, and ethical-social framework, fuel the imminent human cataclysm.

The positivity of abstract thought is understood neither by those who live by it, nor by those who oppose it in the name of a spiritualism devoid of its occult meaning.

The current spiritualism, oriental or occidental, traditional or not, ignores how it bears within itself abstract thought and why it bears it. It ignores being the manifestation of abstract thought—which it thus abstractly opposes.

Those who know what final use to make of abstract thought, are saved—be it the philosopher or the *cowboy*.

***

Rhetoric is the dialectic that ceases to be the ideal form of an external or internal reality, due to the inadvertent arrest of the ideating mediation, or of the immediacy of pure thinking, because the object takes that from which it should be taken: as an object arising for thought.

A scientific investigation can be exact, just like a dialectical analysis; but where their further development is not the connection of concepts arising from the initial synthetic movement—whose *animadversio* (observation) should be the investigator's preeminent undertaking, logical duty, scientific honesty—and therefore does not respond to their essential and organic cohesion, but is the association with which nature operates, replacing the thinking mediation and using for itself the formal relationship, the discourse can be logical and aesthetic, but it does not grasp reality. It is rhetoric.

The inadequacy of science or of logic is precisely the incompleteness of logical or scientific movement at the limit of the preliminary gnoseological mediation, for the fact that they renounce experiencing—as the source of further conception—the synthetic element that has allowed the initial assumption of the data.

For that reason, the data falls into alterity, which excludes the "I," admitting that *quantum* which legitimizes it as an unshakable objectivity—as matter, or as spirit, which on the dialectical plane are the same thing.

***

Dialectics like rhetoric—philosophical or mystical or literary—is the mediation of abstract thought to itself, in that it loses the original mediation and is unaware of losing it, and yet unfolds according to a formal, logical and simply discursive correlation, as if it were thought (itself), but which actually alienates the essentiality of thought.

The correlation is no longer the movement of thought, even though it takes advantage of its energy, in mere reflective form. Therefore, it is nothing more than an empirical association, whose futility and gross nature is concealed precisely by proceeding in the elaborated guise of language, logic and aesthetics, which can assume the tones of wisdom, or of sacredness, or of spirituality—of dialectics.

The correlation can be logical, analytical, aesthetic, symbolistic; however it takes place according to a *continuum* that looks like thought in its actuality, but in fact it is not. It is not the thinking that thinks the various determinations but, rather, the determination itself that, in its mechanical autonomy, is now mediated within itself and consistently asserts its abstract necessity, to which thinking is subjected.

Mechanically, the correlation of thoughts "already-thought" becomes the relationship of the multiplicity of terms or of words, whose value is their definition: therefore joinable not by virtue of thought, but according to a rhetorical assonance, or according to the logical-mathematical connection—in both cases, however, based on an unconscious mastery of sensuality.

***

Within abstract necessity there can always be found a content of consciousness tied to corporeality, such as instinct or sentiment, which has an obsessive character, but feigns its own necessity and authority precisely through verbal wealth, formal structure, and rhetoric.

Now we seek the value of the spirit in the formal element; now we presume to find form in the abstract spiritual value, whereby it is inevitable to fall into metaphysical declamation and spiritualistic parody. Or, we deduce the non-deducible from texts of ancient wisdom or of ancient mysticism or of traditional speculation and, according to an arbitrary comparative philosophy, we allegedly reconstruct historical processes of thought, proceeding by way of correlations between mere names of philosophical positions and correlative dialectics. We trace panoramas of a sublime verbalism, from which it is not possible to draw a single objective thought.

The task of some current theorists of Eastern thought and expositors of Sacred doctrines, is to demolish the ultimate defenses of the spirit's citadel, reducing the language of knowledge and of wisdom to a status of a nominalistic dialecticism or an esoterizing aestheticism, so that it ceases to have meaning.

Dialectics like rhetoric, which presumes to teach the aesthetic art, or philosophy or mysticism, is instinctive thought that does not possess itself as thought and, therefore, does not know the power of its own spontaneity but, rather, that of nature to which it identifies. Its dialecticism, its refined analytics are an expression of a sensuality that continuously has to extinguish the light of thinking and feed on this dead light, to eliminate the inner human being.

The danger of such an error lies in the possibility that the rhetorician of the spirit influences disciples. They certainly cannot divert those (disciples) who through vocation and will are inclined toward a supra-sensory experience but, rather, that wider circle of researchers whose orientation, being less self-determined, demands the proper help, the prudent indication. Those people will have to error a long time, maybe even until death, to understand the deception they have undergone, the sense of the teaching that they have received in its alteration.

The rhetoricians's error is to speak about what they really do not know. But precisely for this, they speak and write. The Obstructer, inspiring their dialectics devoid of idealizing mediation, can come to dominate groups and the multitudes.

It is not so much dialectical error, or spiritualistic rhetoric, that ruin unwary followers, as the "demon" that acts through the false instructor or the false philosopher, by passing into their dialectics. Such a demonic spirit is transmitted, is incarnated and is capable of living for a long time within the soul of the contaminated person.

***

From living thinking one passes to the abstract, not vice versa. Living thinking in a discursive guise becomes abstract.

We do not escape abstract thought. We can escape it only by way of meditative mediation, that is, indirectly, if we move from a non-conscious point in which, by thinking, we still have not yet fallen into abstraction. The art is to allow the forces of ordinary consciousness to operate as mediators of supra-consciousness. But, for this reason, such forces must not have supra-consciousness as an object.

From the known and expounded doctrine of the spirit, dialecticized, we cannot pass to the spirit, because movement is impossible where thought is immobilized in notions and fixes these notions in their discursive reality, unknowingly elevating this discursiveness to a transcendence, upon which it can depend mystically.

Understanding the teaching allows us to understand how the thinking that thinks it has no other task but to grasp itself in the movement by means of which it thinks it, since such movement is more important than the object: in order for the object to be penetrated, not merely reflected.

As soon as thought, normally abstract, seeks a reality, an asceticism, a doctrine, outside of itself, whatever they may be, it cannot help but reduce them to its own abstractness, being unable to distinguish the timeless moment in which it essentially receives them, from the lifeless form by means of which it learns them. Fixing them as an object, it inevitably abstracts them, because it immobilizes them in the reflected moment, namely in their temporary mediation, beyond which only they have meaning: ceasing to be real, if they are identified with such mediation.

The method taught by the Master of the new times enables us to resolve abstract thought within the very process of abstractness, without jumping into myths or into transcendences, where the thinking of which we are unaware projects itself. Disciplines and meditations tend not to fix themselves as the subject of a doctrine to be taught but, rather, to arouse the very foundation of the thinking with which we directly think, namely to enucleate from the immediate argument necessary for daily existence, the thinking that is already alive but unknowing of itself, so that it can identify with its pure movement, or with its latent force—which alone renders possible the survival of the doctrine, the teaching. It is the spirit that teaches, not verbal repetition.

The profound force of the "I" is not beyond, but within the life of thinking. That method is not taught by virtue of exposure, but by the presence of thought within the exposure.

The exercise of thinking, or of meditation, or of esoteric imagination remains a mechanical process, even if diligently carried out, if not supported by the sense of the distinction between abstract thought and living thinking: which is intuition granted by the spiritual world insofar as the movement of thinking coincides with it. It is a coincidence renewed by virtue of fidelity and gratitude.

Those of us, for example, who do not know gratitude, cannot be thinkers, because we ignore the coherence. We cannot be logical, because we avoid *recognizing* in ourselves the source of thought: through what inspirational agreements received at certain moments, the right thought was able to shine in us. Ungrateful are those who ignore what they have received, because they have not known how to guard it.

***

Abstractness is resolved within the very process from which it originates. We must not believe we can escape it by dedicating ourselves to things or to doctrines of existence, because it is in any case the abstractness that in other forms extends its own dominion.

Likewise, spiritual doctrines, learned, become abstraction—being forced to mean something at a level that does not respond to their content. However, unlike any other, it is an abstraction that manifests only to refer abstract thought back to itself, namely to the fabric of its own form, to the awakening of the consciousness of its movement. No other "awakening" exists.

The art of thinking is not technique, nor learning, but the will that arouses itself in the form of knowing, because it is the only one in which it can manifest consciously, free of corporeality. Such will is always the inner force of knowing, but it is never experienced directly, since it is a movement of life that coincides, beyond waking consciousness, with its levels of dream and of sleep. Actually, today, we are not interested in the knowing, but in the known. Therefore, the "object" can dominate us, without us knowing it. The world's materiality becomes the "subject."

The resolution of abstractness is not a mechanical art, reliable in didactic and cultural proceedings. It is an art that cannot be not learned, but lights up to the extent that someone is there to light it up. The method of the lighting up can be learned; nor is anyone forbidden to study and think, so as to warrant that the method meet the art. This (art) is given to those who offer living thinking to the work of the invisible Masters.

Without the resolution of abstractness, the art of the action is lost, since fidelity to the teaching from which it may arise is impossible—which is fidelity to the spirit, not to the expressive form.

Once the art of thinking is lost, no longer is inspiration possible. It is useless to have doctrines, or books, or secret teachings. Sacred Science no longer flows, since it is unable to coincide with the series of notions.

Each time abstract thought seeks the resolution of its own limit outside of itself, it does nothing but further project it, re-enforcing its own opposition to the supra-sensory. It must operate within itself, by means of a movement with which it becomes abstract. Because it can be abstract only after having been alive. Only what is initially alive can die. Only a flame can be extinguished, not what is already extinguished.

For this reason, the secret is the living moment, presupposed by abstractness—namely, the moment with respect to which we are not conscious, we are not awake.

Each thought is born alive, but unknown, and it becomes known, but extinct: this knowledge being once again unknown.

Concentration intensifies the form of abstract thought, until it becomes full of its impersonal content, which—while thereby becoming pure individual experience—has nothing to do with the form that aroused it. It must be said that the authentic individual experience begins at this moment.

Concentration up to this point is possible for anyone—for a dullard as well as for an intelligent person, for a moral being as well as an immoral one. What it can achieve beyond is the art of lifting consciousness from its "neutral" state to an initial stage of life, strengthening the movement thanks to which it already operates as the waking state. It is the art of thinking to provoke, through abstractness, the death of its own abstract being, by leveraging, internally, the element of life, which lights up from such a death—the element of life that is always there because of the fact that we think, but it is continuously lost.

It is an indescribable process because it is only possible as a non-dialectical event, granted by the spiritual world, as a response to the fidelity of thought.

At this point, we understand the importance of passing, as modern rationalists, through the experience of abstractness.

***

Sacred Science, unaccompanied by living thinking, can no longer be understood. But it will be brilliantly expounded, because it is dialecticized. Thinking that was lit up must, in turn, light up, if it does not want to be extinguished. The art of meditation must not be lost by its depositaries, caught up in orthodoxy and in the sacred attachment to the verbal experience.

When thinking is not the same movement with which it intuits and thinks, it always leaves, outside of itself, its own object, which remains apart from it like an unknowable unknown, fixed in images devoid of imaginative life—a subject that it can elaborate only as knowledge. Likewise, in the field of current science, the subject of the world remains outside the knowing act, so that the sense world is assumed as real and consecrated in its alterity.

Certain planners of Sacred Science tend toward a spiritual knowing that exempts thinking, because this knowing is already completed and as such untouchable—orthodoxy consisting in such intangibility, or stillness. They tend to identify precise and definite images that exempt the need to imagine with inner and unpredictable effort, according to what the essence of that Science teaches. If Sacred Science were the truth already fulfilled with its metaphysical counterpart, it would suffice to learn it like a Pythagorean table, but no spiritual movement would be possible in it.

The error consists in believing that in the presence of human knowledge, the spiritual, as an antecedent, is described or motionless in allowing itself to be learned, and it does not express itself in the very act of knowing it. Because to penetrate directly into the immediacy of such knowledge demands freedom and will—which is to say, the love of the idea.

***

It is true that normally we find a reality before us that seems to pre-exist thought, but our art is not to fix it in the immediate being or in dialectical form, and as such, place it in front as alterity founded on itself, forgetting the "I" from which *in primis* arises the possibility of placing and of placing even ourselves; rather it is to understand how we come to know it—thanks to which movement it arises in us as an immediate being, or how it passes into dialectics.

The cultivators of Sacred Science must keep in mind that now—dialecticism having reigned unchallenged in culture, in customs and in the soul—no content of this Science can give what it bears, if the thinking that thinks it is not grasped, or if we are incapable of the devotion that the content demands non-dialectically. The teaching initially leads to the possibility of living thinking; where this living thinking arises, that teaching is revealed to us. In that case, only the teaching gives the content in its entirety. It is possible to abandon ourselves to it, like to a rising current of thought, in intimate reception of the soul.

Orthodox knowledge, in its formulation posited as a condition for inner experience, is the spiritualistic resuscitation of the Kantian noumenon,* leaving the spiritual outside of itself, as not identifiable with the same source of the thought capable of thinking it.

There is no passage from abstract thought to living thinking, just as there is no possibility of imaginative vivification of sensory contents, without the self-perception of thought. This

---

*   noumenon – (in Kantian philosophy) a thing as it is in itself, as distinct from a thing as it is knowable by the senses through phenomenal attributes.

is the possibility of the dedication and the rising of the sacred element in the conscious act.

The real obstacle to living thinking is (thought) already-thought, that which, as a notion, dogmatically posits itself and presumes to function as truth, it being a dead image.

Sacred Science is not the transmission of books, or the repetition of teachings but, rather, the transmission of a life that can never be extinguished, because it is the substance of light that unites one soul to another, one world to another, one idea to another, so that, in order to enter into the dialectical circle, it must first of all be the lifeblood of the expositor's soul.

In reality, expositors can transmit only what in them has been fulfilled and lives as a force of the soul, not what they merely narrate.

***

Those of us who do not realize the distinction between living thinking and thought already thought, cannot understand the distinction between the virtue of human activity (whatever its form) and the completed work, which no longer has a relationship with such an operation: which alone should have an economic value, for the same reason that no economic process should grasp or condition the virtue of the work—as instead happens today the world over, to degrade human labor and kill the sense of life.

Those of us who believe we have the keys to knowledge and are heirs to an art of meditation, should doubt truly possessing this art, not only because of the internal problems within our associative experience of membership, but particularly because of the difficulty in distinguishing the forces that operate in our own community—if, for example, the vital-economic need, or the legal-normative need, occultly determines the internal process of the scientific work and of the associative cohesion, or if the free spiritual element, which arises outside of their schematology, is not only unrecognized by them, but also opposed.

In truth, abstract thought is that which can assume any form, its content not being thought, but nature, egoity, longing. There is no passage from abstract thought to living thinking; where living thinking, freshly thought, or formulated, or taught, is already abstract by expressive necessity. Being an expression, it no longer has a relationship with its source. Such an expression can live again only insofar as thought takes back its life with respect to it, independent of it—such life being the truth.

7.

The Science of Perennial Thinking

We must know the movement for which one thought is drawn from another, until opening up to impersonal thinking.

We cannot perceive such a movement before we are able to concretely rebuild a thought, by means of concentration.

There exists only one thinking—transcendent in its being its own foundatiom. It is immanent insofar as one thinks it. It is thinkable all the way down to its foundation. In other words, it is perceptible in its transcendence, which is more than thought. There is no interruption between the two phases, except for dialectical necessity. This thinking flows inexhaustible, continuously interrupted by the mental (sphere), but ignored by it. In the mental (sphere), its eternity vanishes.

Interrupted, it is estranged from itself. One thing is thinking, another is what is thought. What is thought is the death of thought, despite being the objective necessity of the dialectical process and of culture.

Such a condition, nonetheless, through the spiritual practice of thinking today is the possibility of a "resurrection," if we recognize and experience the death of thinking in its effectualness. We must relive the process of its death. We do not need to be astute thinkers or logicians to conceive such a task and to grasp the ultimate meaning of thought, as a possibility of birth of its supra-sensory content, from the experience of its death. This death, being an continuous event, presupposes a life, continuously destroyed.

This birth contains the germinal forces of the future earth. The death of thought is a fact that we must acknowledge, by making our way through this experience, through the *forces* of logic (not by means of logic)—namely, the very forces of the death of thought, in which its life is hidden.

For the flow of thought to be ours, it is necessary that it not be ours. We must not grasp it. Instead it must allow itself to be grasped by us, so that it can maintain, intact, its richness of life. It is the task of opening up.

For this opening up to be possible, we need to have learned to observe thought, until we have it objective before us, which is the unintentional identification with its movement. The identification with the movement is the independence of thought from the form by means of which it manifests. Then, its formative virtue is expressed in it; the formative virtue is given. The limit of cerebralism is overcome.

Opening up is the act of freedom and of devotion—the highest form of will. Devotion is the mental stillness that awaits, that allows the force-thought to blossom. The force-thought is the identical fabric of the vision and the internal reality of the world's entities.

***

It is important to understand how the movement for which a thought is drawn from another, and this drawing of a thought from the other, are distinct acts.

In having the succession of thoughts, we do not yet have the movement, but its possibility.

The movement is gathered by overcoming the need to follow thoughts in order to recognize their form.

One follows the movement of thoughts, not the thoughts (themselves). The non-corporeality of the movement is a force more intense than the formal movement of thoughts, which is nevertheless needed to realize it.

To get rid of the need to follow thoughts, we must have learned to recognize them without the discursive guise, that is, in their informal movement. This is contemplating, possible to those of us who know concentration. Contemplation is the path to devotion, which we humans have lost and today have only illusorily.

The informal moment of thinking is its formative power at the pure state, which enlivens the virtue of contemplation. It is the unknown presence of the Logos, which emerges and operates from the depths of thinking as the virtue of a new liberated relationship with the world.

The pure experience, which would like to be the fundamental criterion of contemporary science, is viable only as an objective contemplation of thought. The only legitimate realism is the one whereby we let thinking express itself, according to its own spontaneous autonomy. For we are before the only reality that is true as it immediately given; as pure thought. Every other world content demands to be mediated by thinking. Only thought is already real as it occurs.

By an analogous movement, the world can be experienced as pure self-giving in perceiving, insofar as we have it in its immediate encounter with the original manifesting of thought. Here the unity, or the identity, of the "I" with the world begins to rise again.

**

Those of us who are deluded into thinking we can detach ourselves from thoughts in order to contemplate them, remain attached to a thought that we fail to notice. We are further played by nature—namely, by a more subtle realism.

We are played by the thinking nature, the most difficult to discover, because it is endowed with extra-rational power—the one that, occultly unresolved, but nourished, leads to deceitful inner experiences, to pseudo-clairvoyance, to false freedom, to esoteric dialectics—namely, to dignified individualism.

We do not leave the thinking nature, which is the innermost egoism.

Only those of us who know how to give ourselves limitlessly to a thought can escape it, so as to thereby engage the force-thought rooted in the depths of nature and that from there operates as egoism.

To achieve the unlimited giving of oneself to a thought, it is not enough to know the technique of concentration, of which, moreover, an ample teaching is already given by Spiritual Science, whose texts are available to everyone. We must decide to enter into this teaching. Courage, devotion, the will to move beyond our very nature is needed. Courage is to follow a "path" that is not mediumistic, namely a path that demands a change of what we are—not a spiritualistic extension of what we are—and what, unknowingly, we secretly want to remain.

The technique is useful to those of us who do not want only to know, but more importantly to act. Because this acting alone becomes self-knowledge, the possession of one's own nature.

The knowing that is not "acting" is the game of the thinking nature. To act is instead to arrive, indirectly, with the force-thought, at the roots of nature, by intensifying conscious thinking, whose form, initially bound to nature, is resolved thanks to this intensification.

"*Il pensante*" (that which thinks) is the spirit of the already-thought. Nature is the already-thought without spirit. The Logos is the spirit of matter, which operates unknown within thought.

Nature can impose its game, only by taking possession of thought. This thought, by losing its force, becomes rhetoric, the guise of non-being, namely the vehicle of powers adverse to human beings and the prompters of dialectics that feign culture and the spirit—prompters of the form of certain present-day occult organizations, whose process of aggregation in function of hindrance it is important to know.

The spiritual practice of thinking is the only one that can lead beyond the deviation and inevitable betrayal into which we unconsciously fall, insofar as we are played by nature. Until we are capable of such asceticism, we must have the wisdom to control our own path through the advice or the orientation of those who intuit realizing it. But not even such wisdom is easy or gratuitous.

The game of the obstructing forces can be recognized by those of us who have a steadfast will to understand it; any confusion before it being the insufficiency of such a will, namely the ego satisfied with the paralysis of thought, in which it believes to think.

Those of us who want to be free, can truly immerse ourselves into nature, because we know how to immerse ourselves into the depths of a thought. Thought free of the senses is the will that can penetrate the depths of the sensory. Celestial forces flow in such a will, permeating the soul and its relationship with the sensory.

Nature is the great helper for those of us who are not dominated by it, insofar as we understand the extent to which it dominates us.

Nature's dominion over the inner being, in this time of the manifestation of the consciousness soul, gives rise to the possibility that certain occult organizations are strengthened by hindering forces, active there, where the consciousness of individuals is overly bound to the sensory world and to its cultural system. And, at the same time, it opens the passage to the rhetoric of thinking and of the spirit, even where it seems to cultivate a just teaching. It is the reason for which all those with a mediumistic, or pseudo-clairvoyant past must be advised to always doubt their own esotericism.

***

The human being's fall comes to an end gradually—along various cycles of civilization—as the fall of thought into the sensory (realm), because there alone it is fulfilled and, in being fulfilled, it can also give or not give rise to the motion of re-ascension.

Fatal, both historically and traditionally, is everything that occurs for human beings up to this point. From it, however, arises the possibility for us to take on the initiative of our own story, the orientation of our own destiny. The supra-sensory principle, through nature's co-operation, has led us to the thinking capable of comprehending the sensory aspect of the world. Now, we can recognize within thinking the vehicle that reconnects us with our supra-sensory origin, with the very principle of nature.

The concentration of thought, as taught by Spiritual Science, is an achievement that cannot come about only through the knowledge of texts in which the teaching has been reflected, or on the basis of "restricted" notions transmitted by continuators, but primarily on the basis of a purity of heart that we continuously demand of ourselves, as a "measure" of correct thinking.

This concentration differs from all past inner disciplines, because it implements in the form requested by the new times, that of timelessness which belongs to the Tradition. We must understand the purpose of rigorous attention devoid of personal feeling that thought demands for its pure determination and, the ultimate sense of the rationalism of this time, in order to grasp the supra-sensory that operates as an impersonal power in exact thinking.

The concentration to which we allude manifests in order for thinking to so grasp its own movement, as to bring about the possibility of reversibility—which is the perception of the power normally imperceptible, by means of which it has been able to create the scientific systems of the physical world. The impersonality that, as an objective force, characterizes the positive process of science, is a quality that essentially belongs to thought and, as such, can give it a way to be the vehicle of spiritual investigation, if its precise laws are observed.

Only the thinking that is bound to the sensory (realm) and has come to express itself within it, logically and scientifically, to the extent that it is absorbed by its own object, has the *possibility* of perceiving the force of the movement by means of which it identifies with the object, in order to retrace it backwards—thanks to the same force. Only thought that is bound can consciously become free, as long as it becomes aware of the bond, namely of its temporary identification with the abstract sensory (realm).

Thought can only invert a process that it has actually completed, inasmuch as it is aware of having completed it and can grasp itself in the act of completing it. Otherwise, it loses itself in the object. The object devours the human being—as is happening.

True *yoga* can be carried out only by those modern individuals that are such masters of rational thought as to penetrate the depths of its movement. The struggle against the death of thought can be conducted only by the person who knows how to experience such a death, lucidly.

But then it is no longer a question of yoga, but of the liberation of thinking according to the awareness that it can attain of its own bond to the experience of the senses and the possibility of grasping its own act, not by yogic canon, but means of the very canon of its own movement, which occurs through sensory experience— therefore, according to a movement in which all the previous *yoga* is actualized and transcended. Because such *yoga* belonged to a thinking not yet individuated, not yet applied to the physical-mechanical experience of the world, but sacredly aimed at avoiding such an experience.

It is no longer a question of yoga, but of Spiritual Science.

***

The task of concentration is to redeem thought, by restoring to it the movement of which it is constantly deprived, namely its life.

In the movement of thinking the Divine lives unknown. It cannot live in the formal projection of thought.

The movement is thought that we think, but it is not experienced as thinking, because it is involved in the object. Otherwise, it would not manifest. It would not be movement. The object has the power of making thought conscious. This is the ultimate meaning of the object.

But this is our human weakness. We depend on physical or metaphysical objects in order to be conscious.

Movement is the secret warmth of the light that thinking bears within itself, but ignores. The object arouses it so that thinking can experience it: such experience only being able to be, consequently, the communion with the object—namely, that which we are really still a long way from realizing, even if we can picture it to ourselves philosophically or mystically.

Movement manifests by means of the perceived object. The object arises as thought. In concentration, this thought is to be thought intensely, so that it can be grasped free of the object.

The object is color, form, action. It arises as a unity thanks to the movement of thought that summarizes them and therefore is living thought, but it is never had in itself as living. In fact, we grasp only its projection, as something in which there is nothing of the form, of the color, and of the action, but only the reflected image. Each time it is deprived of its life, it is sacrificed to the needs of egoic logic.

The life of things and of beings is had and lost in perception, since perception, in order to be, must become a fact of consciousness, which for now is only reflected consciousness.

Living thinking is one with that inner life of things, which is gathered only in its "appearing" by means of sensory perception.

Living thinking is always unconsciously active in perceiving. Perception arises from a thinking-force that touches physical reality and for an imponderable time identifies with it. Similarly, when we think an object, thinking, for a timeless instant—which escapes consciousness—surfaces in its creative form. But once thought, it is immediately lifeless.

***

We would be unable to think an object if already, within the depths, it did not surface as living thinking. But the living part is instantaneously lost, so that what manifests is only the part that, extinguished, becomes conscious.

Generally, an idea is not experienced, but only possessed reflectively. For this reason, when we today believe we have ideals, whose truth is merely the living part that escapes us, we actually only pursue that of them which dies. It is why ideals, continuously degenerating into abstractions, are not implemented—they have no force. Even the feeling that can be kindled by them is devoid of the force from which it nevertheless moves—it, too, suffering, as a consequence of thought, the evil of reflectivity.

Whenever we have an idea without really understanding it, we tap into living thinking; otherwise we could not have any idea at all. But we only look at the dead reflection. We do not notice the loss of the living moment, because it is not even imagined.

To tap into living thinking, we must find what allows for the birth of the idea. We must tap into that of it (idea) which is *necessarily* alive.

Concentration at first consists in reconstructing a thought through a series of mental pictures which are drawn from the fact that this thought is relived in time. The successive merging of the various mental pictures into a single image is the force-thought rediscovered in the timeless moment, before its unfolding in time. What is already living as thought in the hidden inner being begins to reveal itself as an objective movement of the will.

An unusual will takes effect within consciousness restoring the inner thinking—namely, thinking that ordinarily does not know itself, being engaged and extinguished in the sensory (realm) and altering itself in instinctive forms.

The purpose of concentration is to invert what has been inverted, that is, to restore the relationship between spirit and life.

It is not to make the idea serve the object, but the object serve the idea, because only then do the idea and the object coincide.

For now, human culture is not real. It lacks the living force, because the object subjugates thought: the object that nevertheless can arise only as thought. The object that rules us is the new form of idol. Unknowingly, we today once again worship the lying gods.

The sensory object is merely the means for thought to know its own being: to move within the freedom of its own force, which is the will of which life is woven.

***

The stillness of the cerebral organ can be achieved through pure concentration, in that we can will the movement of a thought volitionally identified with an object to the point that this object, becoming the pure ideal form, disappears as an object: and thought assumes the function of objectivity.

True thought is objective. Therefore, we can unite with it. Only with something other than ourselves can we feel at one. The objectivity of thought, realized, is the discovery of the "I" in its immediate identity.

We are then in pure thinking, on this side of reflected thought, which is always the form of the object, sensory or not. Thought, needing no cerebral support, draws on its own formative force and experiences, as pure movement, its incorporeal objectivity. Such objectivity is given by the subject present within it. The subject emerges only to find itself again as an "I am."

This alone can be called thought, because it is actually had as thought, not as the vestment of the "already-thought," be it even a metaphysical object. Such thought draws on inexhaustible forces, whereas the forces of the cerebral organ have a physiological limit. Their restoration in fact requires sleep.

Mental silence is the sleep of the cerebral organ, willed—namely, the access to the Threshold of the true Earth, where the Logos has conquered the darkness and the light of the "I" is rekindled.

This sleep of the cerebral system is the achievement of the highest wakefulness of consciousness, outside of the corporeal support. The cerebral organ begins to know its own state of death as a profound rest, preluding its astral-divine enlivening.

The profound rest is in fact possible because the "I" perceives it as the mental body's first enlivening from the essentiality of that corporeal death in which it, as a system of nerves, is lying.

***

Concentration must be tension of thought, not of the nervous system. As the positive tension of thought it cannot but be outside of the corporeal organism. Therefore, it is not tension. It is instead relaxation of the nervous system, because it is the suspension of its submission to the blood system.

The cerebral organ begins to have a relationship with the circulation of the blood, in which the spirit rules the soul and the soul rules corporeality.

The sign of the reality of concentration is its ability to unfold without any physical inherence.

In concentration, thought does not tense up, even if by means of this (concentration) a movement is carried out that assumes *in itself* all the thinking energy.

There cannot be tension of thought, under any circumstances. However it occurs, the effort is always cerebral. The effort is possible only because of the initial release of thought from the determinisms of the physical instrument.

In concentration, thought brings about a gathering of itself that tends to perceive its own movement as objective. It then implements its own nature, because the whole of thinking flows into it, the thoughts of all things becoming a single thought that converges in its conciseness toward one thing. World thought is accessed through the simplest object.

Thought's gathering of itself is the implementation of the will to which it continuously owes its movement: now not because of a demand of the physical world but, rather, because of self-determination.

The will that thought normally contains in turning to everyday objects—physical or metaphysical—is a will that continuously annihilates itself in the fact that thinking becomes reflection.

In concentration, this will is not annihilated; rather, it is brought to life within the vehicle of the reflected thought that contains it, being directed at an object.

One focuses on an object, which now is not the goal of thought, but the means for its essential expression, and, through the object, so much will manifests in thought that it can free it from the object.

This liberated thought is the true thinking. Its gathering is the force that alone can penetrate the objects and the subjects of the world, and not just be their reflection.

Until now, thought has inevitably always been reflected thought. Even the most acute, the most logical, the most idealistic thought is reflected thought. Reflected thought is never the truth. It is the thought needed by the life of the ego.

The civilization that bears reflected thought as its own imprint, cannot be redeemed and have life, if within it—at least thanks to very rare thinkers—the thinking capable of penetrating the depths of its own reflectivity does not surface.

Only this thinking can penetrate present-day problems, before which reflected thought is powerless.

Only this thinking connects the spirit with the soul, which, devoid of spirit, egoistically corrupts life; because the spirit that directly enters into corporeality, without conscious mediation, is destructive to the corporeal system by which we exist, perceive and think. And if it does not destroy corporeality, it is because it can easily lead it toward a muscular-animal formation, namely toward the formation of an instrument of aversion and destruction.

***

In order for thought to think through its own movement, unconditioned by the cerebral instrument, it must contain the whole of logic, namely all the connecting power that cerebralism can mediate, and have it to the point of being able to do without this—having itself apart from expressive need.

Logic can be a science useful to the dialectical apprentice and to the person who still lacks sufficient forces to be able to move independently in thought: thought *in itself* being independence.

Logic was the first normalization of the thinking being with respect to its own discursive product, the "already-thought." But for this reason it has always necessarily been the expression of the human mind incapable of grasping its own movement in its living instant.

The very movement of logic, being continuously fulfilled, should have led to the awareness of its limit and of its superability.

The ultimate meaning of logic is meaninglessness. Such meaninglessness governs the life of the modern human being, but it is not recognizable by us, now.

The annulment of its very self should be the culmination of logic. There is no logic that in the forming of itself does not tend toward the annihilation of itself, because, for it, the finite is given only in relation to its own limit—the relation not being the finite, but that in which this finite is transcended.

Outside of such a relation, logic is nothing.

Only the appearing of reality can be grasped by logic in its temporariness, not reality.

Human beings, fiercely logical, cease to be truly logical, because they are imprisoned within a mechanism of thought that leads any subsequent thinking to its own mechanicalness.

Those who discover logic and are exalted by it or place it at the heart of culture, have understood little or nothing of the logical process. They have little possibility of being thinkers.

Logic is form that can only be the form of something, which is thought (itself).

Logic is possible because the ineffable exists.

What can be said with logical clarity—according to what the inspirer of neo-positivism proposed—cannot be the ineffable. Therefore it is not the truth, but only the trace of the living thought.

If logic is formally rigorous, it is however the abstractness that asks to be redeemed into thinking life, independent of the logical formulation.

True logic is the mystery. The language that comes to express it may not be formally delimited, and yet be rigorously logical.

***

The capacity of judgment, logical ability, concern the outer world. They are important for everyday life and for worldly relationships. Before the spiritual, dialecticism ceases to have meaning. But this dialecticism must be there, as a form of a content to be rediscovered. This form must be there, for the virtue of silence to be developed with respect to it. The internal life of everyday logic can be discovered as the adamantine power of thought, continuously lost: the power of inspiration that to be discovered, demands the sacrifice of beautiful speech, the silencing of the illusory word—from which the right word may arise.

To judge, to be logical, or to interpret life is an activity that comes from us, insofar as we have the physical world as an object, or the same spiritual world rendered abstract. Therefore, it is an impediment to the supra-sensory experience, which can occur provided that it flows from what we are not.

What we are not can also be expressed logically at a later time, if by identifying ourselves with it, it flows as our essence.

The physical world can be the object of thinking. The spiritual world can be the object of thinking as long as thought comes directly from the spirit. This is moreover the sense of receiving the contents of Spiritual Science. The disciple receives, by means of such contents, something that springs directly from the spirit. What we grasp as disciples moves from our interiority.

The greatest human intelligence is useless in the presence of the supra-sensory, if it does not have, as its crowning glory, the state of silence, where it has the possibility of its own redemption and therefore of supra-sensory reception.

Dialectics is the death of the spirit. Therefore in the presence of the spirit, it must die, so that the word can arise.

Mental silence is the crowning achievement of a productive intelligence. If this intelligence presumes to interpret reality or to evaluate the supra-sensory, it becomes itself the impediment to experiencing the reality of the world.

Whatever can flow from the spiritual world has the mark of impersonality and, to avoid being altered, demands that the power of personality acquiesce in silence, which is its being actually present to the experience. The force of individuality here manifests its real sense.

Logic, knowledge and human opinions arise from the need to conceive the sensory (realm) by means of the cerebral organ and from the impossibility of doing without it in the relationships of common life.

But this common life ceases to make logical sense and have objective evaluation in knowledge and opinions, despite the universal systematic dialecticism, if we do not know what allows it to be experienced and how it can be experienced. It is the knowledge by means of which we gave meaning to life before we reduced it to rationality, by establishing a relationship with it mediated exclusively by cerebralism.

For us to achieve what gives real value to life, we must transcend the meaning of life acquired through knowledge dependent on cerebralism, namely a knowledge that nowadays grasps only the world's lability and contingency—namely, that which it is not, and yet presumes to be real.

Even the current forms of nihilism, of the ostentatious absence of ethical direction and of theoretical revolt against conformity, against cultural idols, against idealism and mysticism remain expressions of the cerebral nature, no more no less than the error against which they presume to react. They not only ignore how to truly act, but, by deluding themselves into believing that they are escaping from intellectualistic domination and combatting it, they essentially express in a more serious way their dependence on it.

True thinking is that which is capable of rigorous logic, because its movement is free of such logic. In being free, it bears within itself the ideating power necessary to life.

***

In the abstraction of thought, we *virtually* have the principle of liberation from corporeality. But such a possibility is not perceived by us, due to insufficient self-consciousness.

Abstract thought manifests as a negative projection of living thinking, but the possibility of its positivity demands to be recognized so as not to be annihilated. The arid light of thought, willed in its reflectivity, is the initial possibility of independence from the corporeal being.

The most abstract thought—mathematical or logical—in its initial movement, nourishes the soul with instantaneous light and quickly extinguishes it. Depriving itself of its own inner content, in fixing itself dialectically as alterity—which is opposed to thinking—it also partially loses its formal power; actually it corrupts it. It ends up giving shape to the need of the ego, which, bound to the sense world, can only assert itself in its dialectical guise. Nevertheless, such thought, being the principle of extinction of the soul's vital-instinctive element, is the possibility of its pure self-willing. It is the possibility continuously lost, or altered.

At first, the abstractness of thought is necessary for the liberation of the thinking motion from physical and metaphysical nature.

This liberation is what can be subsequently willed, or not willed. But willing in this sense involves intuiting the virtual positivity of abstract thought, which is a premonition of the secret of its being alive before its dying. The responsibility of thinking is not only living thinking, but also the form with which the "I am" emerges from its mystery and expresses itself as a foundation.

The rise of responsibility involves that of co-responsibility. There is no one to accuse, in the light of thought, where the "I" encounters itself as the "I" of others, and knows that the profound identification with itself is nothing but the self-recognition in the "I am" of the other.

The error of others always refers to one's own inadequacy, to the abstractness of the soul's movements, for example, regarding what we believe to be love, which is instead the unconscious pretense of the sentiment that we love to have and do not have, because we are afraid to have it in its purity and wholeness.

The measure of freedom is the objective movement of love for each other, namely the co-responsibility achieved through the noetic penetration of the sense of *karma*. There are no culprits outside of me. There is no need to accuse anyone. Those who still accuse others, whom facts and outer evidence and human law condemn, show that they have yet to discern reality from semblance and that they are subjected to the domination of abstract thought even where they do not imagine.

***

Abstract thought is the exhaustion of the life of thinking, therefore its death in the form of consciousness. Such death must be experienced willfully with the loftiest forces of the soul, since the passage through mental annihilation and darkness are necessary for the ego.

Normally, abstract thought is used as a positive, while positive should be the experimentation of its state, which is a state of death. Therefore, abstract thought is produced and used, but it remains unknown in what it has of concrete, that is, in the secret of its being dead. To realize its death is to enter into the virtue of its non-dialectical weft, that is, into the sense of its self-giving. It is the beginning of a deep rest, in which the Divine manifests.

Abstract thought is true, if it is finally consistent with itself, if it is the zero of psychologisms, of metaphysics, of mysticisms, of luciferic and ahrimanic discursiveness. Lucifer and Ahriman, in fact, can do everything in us when they become our inner discourse.

Abstract thought is true, if it is the point in which we are able to draw the positive from its maximum negativity. Its death, not endured as being, but realized, is the rising of true consciousness. To this end, such death is necessary.

With ancient life exhausted, death is simultaneously the abstractness and the possibility for the blossoming of the new.

New as original.

The exhaustion of the sentient element of thought is, for the thinking being, the possibility of silence, which gives the cerebral organ the power to make of its own death a profound rest.

Such a possibility contains and transcends any *yoga*, because it frees the mental from the breath. It restores to the mental its light.

***

At a given moment, we realize that the ultimate purpose of abstract thought is to cease expressing itself. We must know its dead being. Then, the organic death of cerebralism is revealed as a metaphysical event guarded by the physical being. Its death, perceived, is the gateway opened up to its original glow.

Thought is known as the continuous death of its form. The dialectical form is cadaveric, but it is the cadaver of something that can be had alive, if we are capable of recognizing its death. The extinction of abstract thought is the moment in which consciousness ceases to participate in the death of thought, namely the first moment of the life of consciousness in a thinking that is the pure form of itself, because it ceases to be a dead form of something else, as something other than itself.

Now thought carries out backwards the movement in which its dying occurs. This occurring is positive, because it takes place in the presence of the "I am".

To retrace the movement backwards is not a matter of carrying with oneself (along such a path) the form of the object that is thought.

What is thus realized is the new life of thinking, namely the life from which the spiritual practitioner can draw the light that by now is unknown to the breath.

Abstract thought, exhausted, is the stillness of thought insofar as it is empty: empty of itself. Not for anything else has thought become abstract.

Thought has fallen for nothing other than the experience of the emptiness of minerality—the foundation of every empty structure of the void.

The positive of abstract thought is the beginning of the counter-breath, because it is the transcendent opposition to the inverse light of the breath.

Wherever abstract thought is permeated by its negation, the pure motion of thought becomes consciousness of the point of corporeality where matter crosses over to the spiritual.

***

Binding to cerebralism, living thinking penetrates the sphere of a concrete darkness, which is the lifeless state of the nerve substance. In flowing and allowing itself to be grasped by such obscurity, to be reflected by it, it emerges as abstract thought, as a simulacrum of its living being.

Descending into cerebralism, thinking undergoes the action of negative powers of the earthly sphere, which it instead dominated—and dominates—as prenatal living thinking, when it went elaborating the cerebral organ, so that this organ, already deprived of its original life, could become the instrument of physical and rationalistic experience.

As we have seen, the loss of the original life of the cerebral organ was the loss of celestial nature and supra-sensory vision, symbolized by our expulsion from Terrestrial Paradise.

From the experience of negating the life of the cerebral organ, arises the possibility of dead thought's positive affirmation—as abstract thought.

Thinking receives within itself the element of death that renders it abstract, but it is the secret possibility of its metaphysical penetration into the physical being. Thinking undergoes a death similar to what led the brain to lose its original life; but it is unaware of this situation.

The power of life inherent as a possibility in this experience of death is something that is not to be acquired. Because it is already there, it should simply be noticed. What normally occurs is to be discovered because of the fact that it can be thought logically.

To think, of course, thought needs objects, but the objects are not what count. Objects already thought are nothing, if, through them, thought does not free itself of them, so that their reality—which gives itself in the form of thought—can truly be known.

Thinking ordinarily thinks, ceasing to be in the object what it is insofar as it can think. This non-being should be known as its death. There is no other sense of agnostic sensory thinking.

In such a death, thought can be animated by a life which is not a new event, but a super-human reality inserted into the secret of earthliness, as a power of resurrection, where consciousness descends ever deeper into the darkness.

Resurrection is the possibility of thought, insofar as it dies each time it thinks. It is able to grasp itself only in this dying. It is in the logic of its movement; not, of course, in its abstract logic.

Whoever understands this secret has the key to today's problems and the meaning of the path of future human beings. Our current dead thought does not want a rhetorical transcendence without an awareness of its actual state. It only wants the experience of its actual state, which is its death. Because only from such an experience of death does it come alive with its own life.

If thought is resurrected, the brain ceases to be the instrument of nature. By virtue of thought, the brain achieves the stillness in which it realizes the forces that hold it in minerality—forces that are the supreme faculties of thought, enchanted by the sensory vision of creation.

8.

The Archetypes (*). Stellar Perception

The intangibility of the cerebral organ is the adamantine resurgence of its force. The intangibility is original thinking, which does not need to be thought, to become the life of the soul.

The spiritual practitioner can intuit: "I think and a creative current is in motion in the universe." It is the thinking that is one in every thinking being, identical in every soul, but unknown. It is the thinking that is the power of unity of all souls, continuously flowing alive but impersonal in the single heart and dying in dialectics, therefore unknown as a current of life that moves corporeality and provides light and warmth to the experience of the senses.

Thought that rises again is the one that realizes profound spontaneity, insofar as this spontaneity is its original being. But it is the consequence of its freedom, of the highest act of consciousness.

Through the spontaneity of thought, the Divine enters the human being.

For now, we have spontaneous thought only as an expression of instincts. We do not know thought itself as instinct, as spontaneity, because we abstract, we dampen, we dialectically alter its impetus of life. Liberated thought meets the power from which it arises, as creative spontaneity. Its resurrection is its being free as spontaneity, as thought that encounters things, because it is continuously within them. By achieving the contemplation of thought, we learn from thought communion with the world, because we leave it free. We allow it to shine brightly within the soul according to the inspirational virtue from which it arises.

***

---

* The term "archetype" here is used with a meaning absolutely extraneous to that attributed to it by analytical psychology.

Thought's virtue of inspiration is the same power of movement with which an archetype lives in its terrestrial forms.

It is the movement that allows itself to be drawn by spiritual practitioners in pure perception, or in concentration, or in the contemplation of drawing one thought from another.

By means of concentration, we initially reconstruct a thought and will it with intensity. For a long time, we insist on this exercise, to the point in which we can open up to the inner movement of thought, as to what is given by the spiritual world. Gradually we acquire the capacity to extinguish thinking or to lead it to a stillness that we were thereby able to receive in its movement. A higher willing, essentially impersonal, is then in action, to which devotion and silence open the passage.

Those of us who open up to the inner life of thought—insofar as we abstain (even for a brief moment) from paralyzing it in the conceptual determinations ordinarily needed by egoic existence—can receive the gift of the powers that support the world, they being the thought of the world. Then, we recognize the power of thought (as being) one in all thoughts, whose possibility is continuously present in a single thought, which is truly thought by us—to which we are truly given. We can understand the sense of concentration.

The substance of thought is identical to the force that operates as a formative virtue in every created form. But it is not "thinking the created form" that leads thought to the creating virtue but, rather, following (by means of thought) the workings of the force in the created forms. This "following" is the very movement of the force, aroused, then perceived.

Regarding the created forms, motionless contemplation opens, at the root, the movement of the formative force in thought. Pure perceiving is, in fact, the world's immediate thought, namely the living intuition that needs no dialectical form.

***

The motionless forms of beings and things have no reality apart from what allows them to appear as form. This form is real only as a pure movement, or an internal relation. The form, in reality, is always movement. Our art as meditators is to perceive the movement within ourselves—a movement, which, as the being of the form, always arises within the soul, unnoticed, having a non-spatial value, but with an embryonal impulse toward the restoration of the primordial form.

Within the form, the outer and the inner are a single movement. It is a matter of perceiving it.

Such movement is an inspirational power within thought, which lights up as intuition, in a non-conscious area. It can live conscious as pure thought, but ordinarily it is extinguished in order to be conscious as abstract thought.

Each form seen outside of the power of movement that renders it possible, becomes real through the mechanization of thought. Thought's power of movement is immobilized by the multiplicity of forms seen as real outside of their archetypal reality—because of the Inhabitant of what is lifeless, operating within the nervous system devoid of life and arousing abstract appearance, the source of human mendacity.

There is no earthly thing or creature that is not a sign of a lost cosmic correlation, which, by means of form, asks to be reconstituted within the soul, as a power of memory and of restoration of the earth's Spirit—so that the evil of abstract appearance can be healed and pain permeated with the force to ascend, there, where it is transformed into bliss.

In reality, outside of the movement of the archetype, form cannot exist. Likewise, even what can arise from human beings as a formal creation—of art or of thought—is correlative to its capacity of drawing on the archetypal forces of the soul, where thought is the original virtue of image.

The Spirits of Wisdom, of Movement and of Form give the impulse to human imagining that so rules the personal element as to be able to open it up to the impersonality of the supra-sensory world. Even without knowing it, artists create to the degree in which the Divine is present within them. Without such a presence, we can only create forms devoid of life or that feign life.

Thought loses its archetypal force whenever it ignores its own movement and has cerebralism as an inevitable support. It therefore allows itself to be imprinted by the sensory forms divorced from the archetypal root. The forms are necessarily mediated by the senses; but the inner human, to whom the senses open the passage in the sensory world, must go to meet them. Devoid of this autonomous impulse and, therefore, of its own original nourishment, human imagining becomes merely a subjective fact, devoid of life, even if redundant with expressive schemes and rhetorical power. Art becomes cerebral.

***

The virtue of inspiration that animates thought is the same power with which an archetype expresses itself in its own earthly forms. By looking at these forms, we can give ourselves (in our innermost self) to the movement that always creates them from the depths. Thus, we can know the forces that converge and create in our souls.

The form of what we produce in the field of technology and of mechanics, is the expression not of archetypal thinking—as is possible in magical imagination or in art—but of reflected thought, or thought devoid of life.

The archetype of a machine is always a lifeless abstraction, necessary to us as the mediation to the deprivation of the power of operating directly on sensory forms, and therefore as a relationship with the abstract spatial-temporal simulacra that we assume as real, continuously extinguishing there the supra-sensory element of space and of time.

Thus, mathematical thought is a living current whenever it draws on the Spirits of Form for its intuition of quantity and its encounter with the world. But whenever it coagulates, by expressing itself in formulas and in laws, it excludes itself necessarily from its own movement—which, after all, it rarely now possesses—and enters into the mechanical order, which is the annihilation of its formal power. In reality, mathematicians today no longer have poetic will, or the strength to elevate themselves to pure mathematical thought, but they only have thought that moves reflectively in the mathematical order already made, obliged by numeric correlations of the multiplicity of the mathematical "already-thought." They do not possess the numerating, because they ignore how it emerges. Their attraction toward the already-numerated prevents them from seeing how it emerges.

Nevertheless, the extinct power of inspiration from which mathematical science is born, can be found, if the theorem or the formula are assumed as the object of concentration of thought, which must be able to intensify its own inner life, to resurrect the primal movement from the shell of its abstract formulation.

Human beings that think the forms of entities without ascending to their archetypes, are outside of reality. They live in the cosmic lie, because they allow themselves to be deprived of the vision that is before them. They repel the evidence and believe themselves to be practical, positivistic and realistic.

In effect, we must know the *maya* of an entity's multiple forms, so that the archetype of the entity can awaken in us as our own thinking. Certainly, such thought is not the archetype; the idea of a lion is not the archetype of the lion. But the idea as an act, or a moment of life, can only arise as a movement. It is the movement that alienates itself in the conceptual determination, but it must be there for the idea to be possible. Its death is necessary to its becoming conscious.

Those of us who meditatively experience the idea in its dynamic movement and live its flash of life, recognize within it a power of movement identical to the one for which the archetype is present in its forms and can be thought by means of them.

The idea is but that of the archetype which can arise as human thought. For this reason, the abstract form unresolved in the movement of thinking, can be seen as the abortion of an archetype. All of modern culture is nothing but an immense cemetery of dead ideas, which are nonetheless signs of their recoverable life.

The importance of our presence on earth can be understood, if we comprehend how the world of archetypes can live again on earth beyond the fixity of forms, beyond captivity in the multiplicity of nature, by virtue of the thinking that in its own freedom implements the magic of its spontaneity: in which the archetypal power of the ordinary human being flows secretly. Where the will and spontaneity coincide.

***

Those of us who know the power of such spontaneity, can open up to intense sentiments and to objective sensations, as we bring to them the intangibility of the cerebral organ.

As thought becomes pure immediacy, it allows its own physical organ to rest in the buried mystery of its light.

Emotions and instincts that reach there, where they normally condition consciousness through living processes, now flow into the void. By escaping the ego, rendered motionless, absorbed in the foundation, they are perceived by the "I." Perceived, they reveal the force of which they are alterations. Feeling and willing open up to their own light.

Pain or pleasure, repulsion or longing, appear in their own unreflected truth, not as contents in need, but as forms of extra-human entities that ask to be connected with the "I," to express what they are worth insofar as they structure the world. As forces that feed the "I," they submit themselves to the limitations of the ego, inevitably, in their negative or destructive form: in this lies their positivity.

The intangibility of the cerebral organ is its stillness perceived through the intensity and quiet of thought, all the way to the awareness of the negative power of the ego. The negative force, perceived, is the lofty positivity of the "I."

The stillness, realized, is the mental void. But it is the condition already proper to the occult nature of the nerve tissue. Already, it is in itself physically empty—by virtue of its state of death.

Mental silence is not the experience of this void, but only the initial way to access it.

The death of the cerebral organ, experienced, is its life. To experience such death is to cross the barrier of darkness and of fear, toward infinite freedom. But the experience must always be repeated.

One thing is the stillness of the cerebral organ, another is the perception that the spiritual practitioner can have of such stillness.

In its ontological reality, the brain already possesses this stillness, which is its earthly dis-animation.

Those who come to experience this stillness, or darkness of dis-animation, arrive at the boundaries of life; they contemplate the Threshold of the spiritual, the dawn of the light.

Great healing is contained as a powerful hope and as an immanent reality in the evil that human nature temporarily bears. Evil must become the good that we believe we find in the sensory system.

To realize the stillness of the cerebral organ means to free it of the need to draw life from the bloodstream; to free it of the need to draw life from something other than the spirit, of which—being the profound negation—it is the immanent threshold.

***

The "stillness" of the nervous system is the individual condition that responds to the super-individual movement of liberation.

From the point of view of "occult physiology," stillness means the flow of the life of thought no longer as thought, but as a creative virtue, from outside the body, namely beyond any vital contribution owed to the blood system in the cerebral apparatus. From the transcendent point of view, we can say that it is the moment in which our free determination coincides with what the initiatic transmission demands from us. At this point, we may be worthy of continuing on the path, brought forward by the light of the Hierarchies.

Having exhausted the velleities, the pure intellect becomes the vehicle of a human will that, in its eradication from nature, coincides in several decisive moments with the direction of superhuman willing. It is the moment in which the Master can, by direct communion, approach disciples and arouse in them transcendent vision.

In terms of occult physiology, according to the teaching of the Master of the new times, one must say that the process of thinking is transferred from the periphery to the internal area of the cerebral organ, toward the point where the spinal cord is inserted in that organ.

In the seat of the cranium, whose form corresponds to that of the universe, there is an original and intact point where initiates remove themselves from the evil of nature and bring salvation to their profound inner being crucified in cerebralism, by encountering with the purified forces of consciousness the original light of what, as an ancient human structure, lies aching and dying in that area.

All the suffering manifesting in various forms of human destiny arises from this area. In the magical act of thinking, disciples carry themselves beyond the darkness and pain of fallen human substance, which daily expresses its powerlessness as a dialectical value, but which through darkness and pain points to the path of reintegration.

The transference of inner perception to this area—which makes no physical or spatial sense—corresponds to the movement of living thinking and to its possibility of being, as a principle of freedom, one with the pre-natal will. It corresponds to the moment in which initiates have the possibility of encountering the Being that closes or even opens for them the threshold to the supra-sensory, namely the Being indicated by Spiritual Science as the Guardian of the Threshold.

Experimenters feel that until now they have known nothing about themselves. They begin to know themselves. They look at their own origin and behold their own real being outside of time, because who looks into them is not the being taken by their own image, but the one that can see of themselves the true image. For this reason, they feel they have been restored to their true nature.

It is the point in which we attain the ultimate sense of freedom and, therefore, are able to learn to what degree we are still oppressed by the sentiment of our own person and to measure the capacity of being founded on ourselves, independent of worldly calls.

Self-consciousness leads us, at this point, to measure the insufficiency of our dedication and therefore of the courage necessary to cross the "threshold." Here, we can already look at ourselves, without being afraid to discover what still binds us to worldly values. But a fear can arrest us, namely that of receiving the force, which we had never before experienced.

The sun's spiritual entities have over the long course of time built our frontal lobes. Through them, by experiencing the essence of the physical world, we free the force that moves thought and turns to a source that connects us to an even more internal power, namely that which moves the sun from the sidereal depths, which we can now contemplate, or renounce to contemplate—by measuring our own courage, our capacity of consecration.

***

The drawing of the corporeal from the incorporeal is an alchemy, in which the celestial forces, which were proper to human beings before the "fall" still operate intact. This alchemy is carried out at a point of the head, on which no activity of ordinary consciousness has a grip.

Only the letting go of ordinary consciousness, by the intensification of will, gives access to it.

The corporeal is drawn from the incorporeal at an imperceptible point where it does not oppose the current of the spirit, for consciousness to arise.

At this point of the head where life arises from the spirit, there occurs, by evading consciousness, the encounter of the mineral world's essence elaborated in nutrition, with the pure content of the sensory experience.

By virtue of a synthesis of the spirit's work in the physical weft, matter is restored to its original adamantine being, thanks to an invisible alchemical process in which ordinary consciousness participates indirectly.

Such a process has a superhuman origin, because it was established by the Logos in the human soul, when it began to avail itself of the corporeal vehicle for earthly experience, without nevertheless identifying itself with this vehicle.

The present-day spiritual practitioner knows how such a process taking place in an "area" guarded by profound sleep, can be impeded and altered by forces of darkness or of false light, and how it can instead be knowingly sustained by the will of the free human being.

The question of freedom here ceases to posit itself as a philosophical or intellectual fact, because this willing cannot have as a vehicle but the thinking capable of grasping its own original necessity, that is, the freedom that for now it has only as an abstract representation.

Normally in sensory perception, we receive unconsciously a supra-sensory content, essential to the making of the inner structure. However, being conscious only of the sensory form of perception, we oppose an abstract moment of freedom—which draws from contact with the minerality of the form—to the structural power of freedom stimulated in us by the supra-sensory element of such minerality, but received unconsciously, like that of the mineral made essential through physical nutrition. (The concept of the "unconscious" used here has nothing in common with that of modern psychologies, having only the sense of a metaphysical level of consciousness: of which neither analytical psychology nor psychoanalysis are able to give an account).

***

The "I" can find its foundation for earthly activity only in the non-spatial point of encounter of two etheric currents, between the pineal gland and the pituitary gland, inaccessible to ordinary consciousness. In this center, the encounter of the two essential etheric forces can be the apex of a sacred magic, the crowning of a secret ritual that only the spiritual world accords to fidelity and worthiness. The encounter of the two forces can be meditatively brought toward the form necessary to the "I" by a direct action in the earthly world. Any meditation in this sense is always an indirect way, that moves from the ego.

Here, the limit to meditation is the consciousness that presides over the mineral nourishment of the body as well as of the sense organs, by alienating itself from that alchemical process, because of the need not to obstruct its sublime function. This necessity, established by the spiritual world in human beings, is today ravished by us not through supra-sensory action, but though an opposite action—namely a breakdown of the occult alchemical process. Which is the attempt to open consciousness to an inferior world, by means of psychoanalytical or spiritualistic or pseudo-magical practices, behind the illusory intent of a transcendence of individual limits.

Overcoming the limit is instead an overcoming the darkness of the ego, as a relationship of the spirit with earthly minerality. For this reason, the sense world is continuously offered to the spirit. But no path—psychological or traditional—can give disciples the way to experience the ego's relationship with earthly minerality.

Of this, the ego must know death as its own death, in order to tap into its living content, which is the element of life always unconsciously drawn from the higher "I," because of its transcendent presence at a non-spatial point between the pituitary body and the pineal (body). Such a presence now cannot act within the us, except through our immediate vehicle, which is self-consciousness, whose metaphysics can be taught only by the bearers of consciousness for the new age, recognizable as disciples of the Rose Cross.

Self-consciousness is realized as freedom, insofar as it makes the impulse of the ego its own, namely the impulse without which the spirit would be unable to enter into earthly world.

Access to the creative form of the light—in the magical "center" of the head—is possible thanks to the elaboration of a substance of life, which can be experienced only in the sense world, by means of earthly perceiving and thinking—that is, where we do not undergo the world's alterity and this (alterity) is not translated into spiritualism, but we grasp in it the act whereby the "I" arises and distinguishes itself from the world, since it is already one with it. Then, what appears as the world's "matter" gives itself as the form of light from the etheric body's inner motion of light.

Thought can look at the alterity only with the forces by means of which it has already overcome it. But the problem is to know these forces. The alterity seen as real is a deception. It is true only as a sign of a unitive power barely taking place, which asks for fulfillment in thought and, yet, (is) a sign of the "I"'s initial communion with the invisible forces of the visible.

The world's objectivity is true, but it is such as a category of thinking. Only a subject can decree the objectivity of the object. The distinction is already an act of consciousness.

The spiritual practice of thinking and of perceiving leads disciples to realize, in conscious form, the inner breath that the ancient *yogi* asked of *pranayama*. They discover the element of freedom within the thinking drawn from sensory experience, just as they discover within sensory perceiving the secret vibration of living thinking.

As modern human beings, we find immanent within perceiving and within thinking the forces of the resurrection and we experience their transcendence in the synthesis. Which is the initial presence of the "I" at the encounter of the two etheric currents, whose dissonance is the grave danger of the present-day human being, since it is the opposition of the consciousness soul to the supra-sensory from which it arises.

***

The spirit realized is freedom. Apart from bodily incarnation, the spirit does not have the problem of freedom.

Human freedom does not yet exist. It is barely a representation or an idea, or, in the best of cases, a volitional possibility of thought.

So that it can realize freedom, which it only succeeds in conceiving, thought must have been able to intuit through its utmost logical effort the significance—as an extreme speculative petition—of the philosophy of freedom.

The encounter of the mineral world's essence with the pure content of sensory perceiving, is the work of a will that we can awaken within ourselves, by bringing to an incorporeal level our own capacity of self-determination in the physical world. It is the will that we can extract from the meditation, as well as from the transformation of the most intense pain.

We actualize our freedom, not by tending to free ourselves from a *necessity* of which we are unaware, but by encountering such necessity through sensory experience and by noticing that we cannot encounter it except through thinking. Necessity is necessity only for thought, but only earthliness can pose it to thought.

Wherever the necessity of thought can be met it is the beginning of freedom. One can understand then how the evil that we encounter, the anguish that we undergo, the tiredness of the body, and illness are events that do not require opposition but, rather, knowledge. They require identification with the forces engaged in their manifestation.

Identification is always thought (itself). In the evil that we suffer, in the pain that we bear, in the darkness into which we sink, there is always non-dialectical thought identified with a determined psychosomatic process. Dialectics lacks the force of this thinking.

It is a thinking of depth that is unknown, since it is not had if not so identified, like a pensato* (an "already-thought") having become pensante**(that which thinks), which opposes thought (itself). Without it we would not know about evil. Evil would not have form within consciousness and would lack its capacity to involve the "I." But it is not imagined that such thought exists, since it is identical to sensation, whose alterity or power of negating the life of the soul by means of the soul's forces, is thus accepted as valid.

It is a thinking of depth that we would not know how to think rationally and, therefore, in certain moments we are made to think by pain. All human "facts" can be understood as necessity posed to a thought, of which we are not capable by willful determination.

The occult synthesis of the pure sensorial content and of the etheric extract of the mineral world tends to restore the adamantine body under the sign of freedom that was proper before the Fall. But such restoration demands living thinking, which carries out the synthesis, for the "I."

The "I" is essentially the subject of the whole work, which has meaning and reality only for "someone" who experiences it, through various levels of consciousness. The presence of the "I" begins in the objective sensory experience, in the ability of the disciple to not escape sense experience. It begins to be alive in pure thought—which we extract from it as a celestial-terrestrial synthesis—and in pure perceiving.

No event occurs in the being and in the life of the human, which we must perceive outside of the thinking through which, as an "I," each of us becomes conscious of it.

Thus, evil is the sign of a latent force to which we nevertheless open the doorway.

Evil is our soul-bodily relationship, altered by the ego, which obstructs the flow of the perpetuity of life in the etheric center of the head, whose virtue is opposed with the abstractness of

---

*   pensato – what has been previously thought: the already-thought, or thought "already-thought"

**   pensante – thinking in the act; the light of thinking in the act of reflecting itself; (See: Translator's Note in *The Light (La Luce) : An Introduction to Creative Imagination*)

thought, while it secretly opens up by means of pain, sickness and death.

***

We know of each illness by means of the head, insofar as we are awake.

Each physical illness is a small experience of death, from which a secret element of life tends to awaken.

Illness is a profound state of concentration of the original forces toward a higher form of consciousness, required by corporeality, namely a concentration that is not perceived as such and of which therefore we cannot feel ourselves (being) the authors, but (which we) unconsciously oppose. Opposing it is the true illness.

Our art should be coming to feel ourselves as the authors of such concentration.

Illness can be encountered within the forces that, naturally opposing a given physical disharmony, bear the balancing power of the "I."

Illness is a magical work of restoration, of which normal consciousness is not capable. If it were directly capable of it, illness would not be necessary.

In feeling ill, we endure the fear of having to be an "I" in corporeality. We fear having to be independent from corporeality. We fear being the bearers of healing, of having to move to a genuine level of independence from organic necessity, namely to a level thanks to which the organism can resume the autonomous capacity of edification.

Organic necessity arrives at illness, due to the absence of independence from it.

Fear and illness are identical, underlain by deep concentration, ignored.

One is ousted from this concentration; for this reason, one feels ill. One is excluded from the healing process. In reality, the illness is withheld, while in another part of the being, one struggles to eliminate it.

If one moves to this profound concentration by means of disease, one becomes a participant in the spirit's creative process.

The ultimate sense of illness is to steer the forces of consciousness toward an autonomy from life-bearing nature, which allows them not to destroy life in order to operate in nature, namely in order to operate according to the spirit of the earthly world. The spirit burns nature to penetrate it as self-consciousness; the excessive, or insufficient combustion generates two types of illness, or it is reflected in their alternate coexistence in the same illness. Therefore, the art of the physician is to gather the sense of the forces in movement by their configuration with respect to the interrupted rhythm, of which each symptom of illness is signpost.

***

Physical illness needs to express itself in the form of sensation and mental picture in order to matter. The content of such perceiving and mental picturing is imposed by a sick body. But we need to understand how, in that case, the instrument of the representative and sensory activity seizes the soul, to give knowledge of the breakdown, not so that the breakdown can spread by means of it, as normally happens—not to have from it its passive acceptance, or justification, or nourishment.

If one is ill, one still has discomfort, whether or not the illness is known. Discomfort cannot emerge without the movement of thinking. It is after all a sensation, which manifests wrapped in substance-thought.

We must insert ourselves into this non-dialectical thinking, so that healing forces can be met in its inverse direction.

The form of illness, for which the discomfort can be felt, is woven of the same force-thought that can heal it. This form can be known as the needed projection of the sick person's interiority. This means that what can know it is the deepest thinking, capable of obtaining the content required by illness; (such thinking) can penetrate it, because it is something more than the form with which it clothes it and with which illness, thus configured, imaginatively received, becomes known in the organism.

It is not a matter of opposing illness. Thought must not combat illness, depending, in its eventual reaction, on evil itself. It must rather converge in itself, to realize the autonomy that is its effective nature, independent of physical processes, by drawing on its original virtue, which alone can connect—by way of the mediation of celestial entities—with the force-thought, subconsciously operating in the organism that is ill.

The force-thought that operates unknown behind the physical presence of illness, can be met by conscious thought that knows, in spite of the illness, how to enter the interiority of itself. A light of imaginative life is evoked through illness by the inner formative being of destiny. Such a being edifies its own earthly figure, transforming into a force of love the capacity to support the obscurity of earthly illness and to bring to it the light of thinking.

Each illness is a profound concentration, in which restorative forces are recalled. They are forces of the higher "I" that tend to enter life, and they can penetrate it, only from the depths of the soul unknown to consciousness, thereby shaking the very foundations of life.

Illness is the vehicle of health.

***

Illness is a profound concentration that we instinctively resist, unknowingly—the ego being what sickens the body. It is important to know how to meet such concentration by means of thought that converges in itself, or to know how not to oppose, or to open up, if the meditation has not been dialectical.

To open up to non-willed concentration is the transcendent meaning of illness, by making this (illness) appeal to mental emptiness, whose opposite is that which holds back illness. In fact, mental emptiness is in turn a deliberate concentration beyond what, as physical illness, compels willing.

We suffer, we fear, we are ill, because we are incapable of identifying with this void. The task is to tend to it by means of memory, or image, or profound quietness. The fixity of the illness can be a helper, in that it teaches the art of insisting on right thinking.

With ordinary consciousness we repel the negation of illness, already underway as suffering. Such a force of repelling can be inverted, if it is recognized.

The rebalancing forces are the same ones that, from the depths, enable mental concentration to oppose its emptiness. But non-opposition demands the perception of this concentration, organically profound; because to perceive it is to bring it to fulfillment. It is a supra-sensory act.

This concentration is organically profound, because it is not willed. It has the force of impersonality and of the relationship of individual *karma* with the karma of the human community. It is willed in the inner zones where the ordinary will does not reach. It arrives there, by ways that the spiritual practitioner learns to know, being the ways of liberated thought—the ways of health.

The human being is a sick person on the path to recovery.

9.

MAGICAL CONSCIOUSNESS

The will that is never expressed in the life of human beings, can arise in the meditating thought. It can free thought from cerebralism, since it is the will from which thought emanates—the true support of thought. (It is) willing that expresses itself in the vehicle of thought.

In essence, thinking and willing are one. In dialectics, thinking separates from willing and annihilates itself as willing. In order to manifest discursively, it must lose its internal force. But thought can realize the autonomy of its dialectical movement, precisely by means of the dialectical process. It can perceive that annihilation and draw on the willing that is nevertheless inside of it. It then perceives willing as its own real support, namely the support with which it can legitimately identify—being one with it, in the "I."

Even when it is not conscious of it, human thought is willing that thinks. It is thinking that creates in a sphere where it ignores its own being. The intensity with which we think is what operates in the world, not the discursive or conceptual form of thought. But such intensity ordinarily comes from nature, whereas it should be the intensity of the spirit. In reality, what we truly will, either through longing or through desperation, or by means of the will that has the force of longing and of desperation, is what is realized in the world.

True thinking is the one capable of edifying the human being, not the one which, in order to be, needs the brain's vital processes. Not the one that even doubts being itself the one that thinks, insofar as it supposes to arise from the bodily matrix, thanks to a force other than the one by means of which it thinks.

Those of us who want to be such, know the willing by means of which we will within thinking, and edify ourselves with thoughts that express our original nature. We cannot help but feel aversion to prosaic thought, to trivial thought, which, although necessary to the relationships of ordinary existence, should have such an awareness of itself as not to presume to be the interpreter and director of life.

***

In the meditative experience, the thinking that discovers inner willing as a support, ceases to have the cerebral organ as a support. It realizes its movement as it really is, in its infinite freedom—supra-sensory. Then, the real is revealed as supra-sensory. The world expresses its true nature.

Reality reveals itself as supra-sensory. The perception of it is not an event that proceeds from nature; rather, it is possible thanks to a will that overcomes nature, operating in its fundamental nature, where it is not yet nature. The overcoming occurs, therefore, without opposition to nature, but by virtue of a death of that which is bound to nature in the soul.

This death is simultaneous with a resurrection that cannot manifest in any other way than with the contemplation of nothingness, or of the non-entity of all that which, as earthliness, presumes to be valid for us. The world's reality can be experienced only through this noetic annihilation of semblance. The resurrection is articulated in thinking, that is, in the supra-sensory act to which nothing can be opposed, since it leads each object or content back to itself.

Being pre-dialectical thinking, or the power of thought—one in the human being and in the world—the spiritual practitioner perceives its movement as an identical presence in the whole of human thinking. Each one thinks the banal everyday life, but what we actually will in such thought moves in the universe.

Without thought, we would not be able to conceive the foundation, which is the foundation of thought and of nature.

Thought can find the foundation in the will that is inside it, unconscious. This will is not separate from thought, rather it is one with it: one might say an internal and intense thinking, magical in itself. It loses its magic by becoming personal or dialectical thought. While emanating from will, personal thought is not conscious of it. Therefore, it assumes cerebralism as its normal support, only because it arises from the cerebral mediation.

Cerebral mediation manifests only to eliminate itself. But that this happens is the possibility of thought that knows how to will the will by which it in essence thinks, until actualizing the death of dead abstractness, which is an operation, not a dialectical fact.

This possibility differentiates the path of the new times from the past methods of the East and the West, which belonged to the Tradition and today are unable to reproduce its movement—the Tradition being neither the method nor the doctrine.

***

One thing is to leave the cerebral support, another is to find, beyond the cerebral organ, the support of the will, which is the path of the human being of today.

To free ourselves from cerebralism and not to grasp the function of the will inside of thinking, means to lose ourselves on a path of the *medium*, and yet to talk about magic, or alchemy, or yoga. It means understanding neither Tradition nor Evolution. The "re-ascension" or reintegration of human beings, cannot be a mechanical fact, realizable thanks to a method that envisages, by way of logical distinctions, the identification of the "primordial" legacy and the plan of ritualism necessary for its restoration, but, above all, the capacity of communion with the mystery itself of the reintegration, beyond every doctrinal reference.

If one does not want to oppose the virtue of the "re-ascension," the importance of identifying metaphysically or perceiving internally the motion of the forces that rendered the "fall" possible, must be understood—so that the new element, ulterior and unforeseen of the "re-ascension" can be recognized, that is, received despite its *inconceivability*. The initiatic art is indeed to intuit how we can open within ourselves the threshold to what is *inconceivable*, because it is real in the depths of the soul—real, severe, and engaging all existence, apart from the vain cultural-esoteric tinkering.

The initial liberation of thinking—possible, according to the method of Spiritual Science, to any modern (human being) capable of thinking consciousness—gives a way to grasp the meaning of death and of the resurrection of thought, as a sign of an event vaster than death and the Resurrection, which, having been completed cosmically in earthliness, can be realized in the depths of the disciple that encounters it through courage and freedom. Such is the sense of finding the support of the will, beyond the cerebral mediation.

Prior to the possibility of such an event, thinking and perceiving, for the human being of the Tradition, were vehicles of individualistic degradation, which they technically had to silence. In them, instead, we can discover the *immanence* of a *transcendent* power, which is our ability to release from the sensory, where its force—in the lower form of traditionalistic-technical culture—goes on manifesting, separate from the principle.

In the depths of objective thought, disciples today can find, immanent, the light that for human beings of the Tradition was transcendent, namely the light that in the beginning contained human beings and was their life—namely, the light that shines in the darkness. In the most individual thinking, we have the possibility of the beginning of reintegration.

In traditional disciplines, thinking, as individual thought, tended to be annihilated in a spiritual object, so that the non-individual forces of feeling and of willing, beyond the immediacy of the rational process, could manifest themselves. This process was known as the movement that tends to bind the "I" to the sensory world. It did not yet know its own reflected organic nature in dialectics.

Spiritual practitioners of today turn precisely to the thinking that connects them with the sensory sphere, being immediate to them and the principle of mediation. Such thinking, by giving itself to the sensory (realm), as can take place only in the modern-day rationalist, is stimulated to draw from its own internal structure, a will that it would otherwise not be able to activate.

The bad thing is that this will remains unknown. It is used, but not possessed. In its earthly aspect it is that power of arid individual willing which brought forth the culture of the machine.

It can be known as the initial life of ideas and as the force that moves from within corporeality.

Thought, separated from the internal life of this will, is modern dialectics.

***

Ancient ascetics did not need to produce such willing, because it was present and evocable in their system of forces. They had to know only the art of encountering it in the psychophysical organism where it flowed directly. They tapped into the profound virtues of nature, to whose power they had not yet rendered extraneous by the rationalistic-sensory experience, as instead should have happened for the modern human being.

Having cerebralism as a support and herein realizing the solitude of consciousness is for us today a condition of the loss of knowledge, but simultaneously the beginning of a new possibility, namely that thought, drawing on its own inner will through sensory experience, discovers within itself the support. By means of such thinking, the "I," as the individuating power, enters the world, It is the chance for us to be able to recognize the meaning of the incarnation of the Logos.

Volitional support is not "external" to thinking, like cerebral support; but thought has had to depend on cerebral support to exchange it for its own, that is, to actualize independence from an exhausted metaphysical "direction," and yet persistent in its formal projection, to give itself to the physical experience of the world and to produce a culture in conformity with the new narrow individualism—which is not true individualism, since it is exclusively founded on bodily needs.

With independence virtually acquired, thought should have found the support in itself, having it by now internal to itself. The support, in fact, is its own being, namely that which truly moves thought, even its erroneous forms. Therefore, one can escape the mistakes of thought only by means of concentration and meditation. Discovering the substance of thought, one discovers the truth.

The true interior of thought can be discovered by those who actualize thought, because this Truth, as the light of the Logos, was one day incarnated in a human being.

What originally moves thought cannot be grasped by means of its dead product. Therefore, no human intelligence can understand the mystery of the Resurrection.

If we are satisfied with the dialectical product, we are not aware of the degradation to which the thought that we are still capable of thinking, subjects itself. The positive possibility proper to present-day thought is lost, insofar as it is free of transcendences, of connecting itself, by way of its free act, with the creative source of universal thought. This universal thought, by virtue of the sacrifice of Golgotha, has joined with each and every human soul and, within it, is secretly the germ of a new life.

Since the barrier of the cerebral support, which continuously makes thinking the reflection, is ignored, everything is mediated by reflectivity: the spirit, religiosity, knowledge, yoga. Christ then operates unknown, by radiating through the darkness of suffering.

By ignoring the light that shines in the being of thought, we ignore how reflected thought becomes the opposite of the spirit, or the opposite of the light from which it is born. Therefore, we cannot grasp how much the present culture opposes the rejuvenating forces that spring from the greatest sacrifice made by the Divine within the human being.

It is necessary that someone know this, if such a culture is to survive. Someone needs to carry out the right investigation, the only one not enslaved to the sensualism proper to each human activity (even the cosmic order is presumed to be reduced to categories of the senses, to something measured and photographed), if, beyond building a civilization, one feels the need to know the inner faculties engaged in its construction and their supra-sensory source; if, in homage to the presumed logical and scientific rigor, one wants to know the nature of the soul forces, which, expressing themselves intellectually, render possible the realizations of science and technology, namely forces to which, alone, one can ask for guidance for that vast external phenomenology, which has lost its human meaning.

Such phenomenology indeed has its philosophizing, but insofar as it is projected there with the power of its mechanical necessity and of its contingency.

***

That which was the virtue of vision and sense of eternity in the Edenic era, is present in us today as the possibility restored to us in an unconscious "area" of the head system, in a center of ancient light, so that we, in another "area," can realize it in a lower form, as the consciousness of the "I." Such is the sense of modern rationalistic consciousness.

The current of willing can be experienced as a magical force. By the term "magical," we mean neither gratuitous psychism nor superstitious ceremonialism, but that of which the will is able beyond the limit that it unconsciously sets for itself.

The emergence of magical willing is the restitution of an original status.

What in this direction appears new, because it is beyond the limit, is in reality original. We can discover it, because we manage to reawaken it as memory, since it is secretly returned in us, there, where its purest being coincides with the "I am," as with a "transcendent" in which we are but still in a state of sleep.

The current of willing can again become food for human life, wherever we, by liberating the force-thought from dialecticism—even from the spiritualistic one—experience the encounter of forces drawn from the skeletal-nerve system with those drawn from the blood-muscle system.

The capacity to represent and conceive must be joined with the profound forces of willing. The spiritual practice indicated by the Master of the new times leads to this.

In mental picturing and in willing the metaphysical polarities—masculine and feminine—of the human being are respectively articulated.

With the synthesis of willing and mental picturing in a single inner act, we restore the life in the soul to the original androgynous element. The path of free imagining and of pure perceiving are always a synthesis of willing and of mental picturing.

The original human being had the two polarities as a single harmonious force, which permeated corporeality.

The separation of the androgynous element into the masculine and feminine polarity points to the loss of the spirit's power over the physical being. But it is also the separation of life from the spirit, namely the separation of mental picturing from willing, therefore the beginning of the era of reflected thought, whose ultimate consequence is the materialistic monism of modern human beings.

The animality of the natural functions is the inevitable consequence of the separation of the sexes, due to the prevalence of the earthly element over the celestial element in the human structure and the necessity of this to adapt to the laws of earthliness, which it originally ruled.

The blood system's opposition to the cerebral system, the encounter of these two systems in an unconscious area, due to the need of the ego, is a sign of the insufficiency of the inner life with respect to the physical one, resulting from the loss of the original androgynous element—whose secret the soul in its inner substance nevertheless safeguards.

***

The animality of the functions of nature is the consequence of the impotence of the original androgynous principle with respect to corporeal life, the lost relationship of the feminine element with the masculine element in the human interiority.

Only an androgynous power, resurrected as a synthesis of thinking and willing, decides the formation of the soul and its future destiny. Egoism does not belong to the soul, but to the "I" that identifies obtusely with a masculine or feminine corporeality. The soul is forced to operate according to egoism, but it is not the one responsible but, rather, the "I" that does not know how to distinguish itself from it, due to the inability to will in thought and to think in will.

The animalistic necessity of sex confirms each time the loss of the spirit's power or of the androgynous principle, over corporeality, which gives rise to the human type prevalent today. We humans, in fact, aimed at being valued only in the physical and sensual domain, essentially establish values of life on the condition of the "fall." All "progress" is mobilized for such values: every struggle, every war, every intellectual activity.

Human civilization must continuously crumble. This is its logic. Each time it is built on unreal or transitory foundations, its destiny is a catastrophe.

Such a civilization cannot again become sacred with traditional props, but only by means of its transmutation: if those called upon do not reject knowledge.

Human evil is certainly not sex, but the unconsciousness with which we undergo the subtle domination of this and other functions of nature, by assuming them as real in their bodily affirmation. This affirmation, in its exclusivity, is precisely the form of our renunciation to know their reality. Therefore, it is our submission to longing.

The secret of sacredness is the magic of willing that again becomes the current of the "I" in the blood, thanks to the converted forces of thinking.

That which is separated awaits to be reunited. It is the demand of the most severe events. The error is inevitable; civilization cannot be but contingent and fleeting, if the inadequacy of the foundation is unknown. Life cannot exist without the spirit, nor can the spirit exist without life. Thus, absolute virility does not exist, just as absolute femininity does not exist.

The category being metaphysically one, as a synthetic power of the dual masculine-feminine force, virility as a specific value is a deficiency. It realizes its own value if it is also femininity. It becomes true by implementing its opposite: its complementary virtue. The same goes for femininity. It must be very clear, however, that it has nothing to do with sensory categories or categories inherent to physical corporeality but, rather, with inner virtue.

By restoring the will to thinking and the light of life to perceiving, we resuscitate the original androgynous element, as the germ of a future human type.

This resurrection is not necessary in that part of the human being where it is already completed. But where it is completed, where we humans bear within ourselves, intact, the forces of Eden, we are not present. Our consciousness is excluded there, where willing is articulated as a force of life, namely in the corporeal structure and in the movement of the limbs.

***

Our limbs are of such workmanship that, in the impersonality of their functional enlivening, they participate in the work of the gods. Our whole being participates in such work, but in the limbs the presence of the gods is expressed directly, therefore in the deepest unconsciousness. One catches a sign of it in movement.

The movement of the limbs is something more than a spatial expression. As such, it is merely a force. But we can understand the inner meaning, or depth, of this force, if we distinguish its invisible being, which is its reality, from its external reflections, by which it illusorily becomes identified.

Movement is at the human being's disposal, but we do not know what it is. It springs from the supra-sensory world to encounter what the free individual can give it as an object. But what matters is its force, not the object. We can will in a will that moves the world's materiality, but we are immersed in profound sleep with respect to it. We believe we are the ones that move the body.

In the force of the limbs, we can witness the manifesting of cosmic thought, which has the power of moving the earth's materiality. Such a force lives in the depths of thinking.

What originally supports earthly life flows in the limbs as a driving power. This power can barely be thought, but it is only reflectively present in thought.

In the movement of the limbs, the spiritual practitioner can contemplate the dynamic light of willing, as it hides behind thought, it being the power that continuously negates itself in it.

The world's creative force manifests in that extremely simple phenomenon, which is the movement of the limbs. In it we can intuit evidence of the Logos. With such movement, we can (do) many things, insofar as we think according to the inner force of thinking, by realizing the synthesis of the dual polarity—masculine-feminine, will-thought.

The Logos that fades and darkens as the human word, flows supra-sensorily in the movement of the limbs. Here the expression of the Logos can be contemplated meditatively, since this contemplation inverts the negation of the light and carries out the androgynous synthesis.

The movement is not something that can be perceived by the ordinary human being. The one who perceives the movement, would enter into contact with the force of lightning. We actually perceive only the sensory reflection of the movement. We gather its outer or inverse sign. We do not move within what moves but, there, where it is moved. We perceive and grasp its moving as a fact.

Only the person who can perceive the supra-sensory can perceive the movement. Nevertheless, the person who meditates can think the will of the limbs; (only the person who meditates) can contemplate this "willing thought" in the limbs and encounter, by means of its inner movement, the force that moves the world.

Before such contemplation, human willing, while arising from remote areas of light, is immersed in the sleep of materiality and diverted toward animality, through the functions of nature.

This animality is not to be ignored, but known in its obscure necessity, where we can arrive only by virtue of the incorporeal will that penetrates the willing which is ordinarily grasped by such animality. Those of us who evade nature, egoically feed its animality. Those of us who know how to advance solemnly, consecrated to the spirit, can enter the magical cavern of nature and know by means of it what has fallen into the sphere of longing and of sexual duality.

***

Corporeal tension, muscular tension, tension of the nerves, objectively observed, always refer to a tension of the cerebral organ, in turn, traceable to an irregular adherence of the mental being to the system of the nerves.

Corporeality as such knows no tension: not even the system of the nerves, as far as its objective structure and the correlative function are concerned. The inherence of the psyche to such a system, because of the curbed insufficiency of reflected consciousness, namely of the consciousness devoid of spirit, is recognizable at the origin of every tension.

Tension is always the contradictory exertion of the spiritual element in corporeality, as either too detached or too gripped by corporeality, because of the lability of reflected consciousness.

Therefore, it is unable to set into motion what it really is. It lacks the soul environment in which to activate its supra-corporeal virtue.

The spirit does not need effort.

Whoever knows the stillness of the cerebral organ, knows true rest, because the physical body, in its structure, in its substance and in its function, does not know tension.

Tiredness is always tiredness of the nerves. Muscle strain due to physical exertions is the incapacity of the muscular system to tap into the force directly at its own source, given the interference of the nervous system, necessary to consciousness. For this reason, we believe muscle development to be necessary, as if from this comes strength.

Through the sense of corporeality and the sense of movement, consciousness,—partially aware of itself—has the illusory sensation of being the one that moves the body, while in reality it represents the movement to itself, which is carried out by impersonal forces that it is unable to perceive, given their supra-sensory nature. Their perception would be possible to consciousness thanks to a higher level of activation of its own individuating power—a power that, instead, ordinarily escapes them, by manifesting in the lower form of bodily tension. Therefore, it has only the perception of the sensory effect of those forces. It does not know the movement but, rather, what is moved.

We humans believe that we move the body. In reality, we automatically give mental commands to ourselves, which are simple mental pictures. We thus solicit a dynamic system that functions all the better, the less we intervene in it or delude ourselves of intervening in it. For us, in reality, a positive task is to know the relationship that we have with such a system, there, where we are one with ourselves in consciousness, so as to arrive through incorporeal imagining at contemplating the *objective autonomy* of the force that we solicit in the limbs.

We can realize within ourselves the force that moves the limbs, if, by intensifying the life of thought with which we ordinarily think, we come to distinguish—as a spontaneous power of image—the representation of movement from movement as perception.

It has nothing to do with rational distinction, but with a noetic-perceptive distinction, which can also become a logical distinction.

To exercise such a distinction does not have to be the paralysis of movement's natural correspondence to thought. Rather, as a movement of imagination, it cannot but operate in the current of spontaneity.

Perception and thought here are an identical act. The spiritual practitioner knows the identity of the forces immanent to thought, with the being that ordinarily seems real beyond thought.

Those of us who understand that distinction, can picture for ourselves the force that moves the limbs; we can think in the limbs the power of the world. Thinking opens up to its primordial life, having it as life that in the limbs is the movement of the light—the light of space.

To imagine the impersonal will of the limbs, spiritual practitioners evoke the will within thinking. They evoke the force within thinking, namely the will by which we ordinarily think, without nevertheless possessing it—the will that does not depend on the cerebral support, even if its movement is in relation to it, or to corporeality.

To discover this will is to give the foundation back to thinking: the "I am," which frees it of its reflected condition, but likewise, gives it the strength to imprint the spiritual into the life body, despite its closure within the bodily organism.

***

The metaphysical force of the limbs can be contemplated as being free from the system of the trunk.

The force of the limbs cannot be conceived imaginatively except as the current of life independent of the trunk system. It is drawn directly from the superhuman (realm). To contemplate it is to elevate human imagining to the impersonality of vision of the Hierarchies from which it springs.

Any pressure of the will of the head or of the functions of the spinal system on the limbs, is contradictory. It is continuously possible, even if meaningless. It is always inane tension, which in the long run alters and destroys the metabolic system; it annihilates the physical foundations of life.

The autonomy of the spinal cord is not achieved unless it agrees with the force that is profound and dissimilar to it, which is the autonomy of the limbs.

This autonomy can be known through the power of image, since in imagining it draws from the same force.

The current of light that can flow in the limbs is all the more original the more it is realized as being extraneous and different from the system of forces of the head and trunk.

The more the limbs' will forces become independent of the system of the trunk, the more deeply they penetrate the radical nature of the longing to which sex is bound. Here, we encounter life as the force that comes alive with the purifying of itself, or by freeing itself of the personal element that unconsciously compels it.

Movement is the power of image that occurs as the perception of the being of the will. Precisely for this, it can be evoked imaginatively, without involving body mobility but, rather, on the basis of calm stillness, of calm contemplation.

It is the flow of the incorporeal will, which normally is realized in its impersonality, as a movement of the limbs, having its organic seat in the metabolic system, where it prevails as the metabolic power and the foundation of every corporeal chemism, binding itself nonetheless to the radical necessity of the ego in the physical being and, thus, becoming food for the instincts.

The essential force of willing surfaces in an "area" of the head, by means of an *incorporeal center* and yet with a definite location, from which it pours out as thought. It operates as the creative power of thought, but without being dialectical thought, which we ordinarily know, and which becomes such at the point where it separates precisely from the source of the force—which, in fact, operates *behind* the area in which thought becomes self-conscious. In reflected consciousness, thinking extinguishes, dialectically, the life of willing that allows it to express itself. This self-expression, as we have already seen, is continuously the death of the spirit.

The essential force of willing is the resounding, within the human structure, of the primordial light of life that the cerebral organ has constructed in order to manifest as thought.

Through the being that becomes aware of itself in thinking, such light of life can be discovered, as long as we know that it dies in thinking and that anything—physical or metaphysical—which this (thinking) conceives, is dead. And that we do not escape from this death of thinking by way of any traditional provision, but only by working through dead thought to know the process of its dying, because in this (process) its life is gathered.

***

If the soul were educated to its true relationship with the muscular system, this (system) would acquire, by conscious virtue, ever greater autonomy of its own movement. Its force would tap more and more directly into the metaphysical source. It would be a further experience of the soul.

Consciousness is insufficient in its relationship with corporeality, since it is consciousness reflected by the physical organism. For this reason, it tends to lean more on the immediate support (the body) than on itself. It thereby prevents itself from having an objective relationship with the body. It oppresses and destroys the body.

The autonomy of corporeality does not result from a diminution of consciousness, but from a strengthening.

And so, eurythmy is the art of reconnecting the movement of the body and of the limbs, an individual manifestation, with the rhythms of the cosmos, whose life surfaces in space—as movement. Thought that wills in the movement of the body and of the limbs in space is reunited with original thinking. Therefore, movement tends to express the original word out of which the corporeal being is born.

Eurythmy cannot be technical. Wherever it is only technical, its art dies and the forces of movement projected into corporeality by way of reflected consciousness, become destructive.

The art of eurythmy is initiatic. It does not suffer profane adaptation, or scholasticism, since it can be transmitted to disciples through ordinary teaching, provided that this, in the person who teaches, is the vestment of a content that flows by super-individual virtue.

The transmission of the art is not technical, but the virtue of teachers who in their work take advantage of the technique, as of a living form, whose soul is the very rhythm of corporeality in the incorporeal moment, namely the movement. The original movement is not spatial, but by means of the mobile figuration of the human form, it enters into space and, thanks to the individual consciousness of space, it can flow from the cosmos onto the earth, bearing the lineaments of a superhuman willing.

Eurythmy is the immediate deep meditation, but traced in figures of light and of space. It is the meditation that does not give rise to knowledge or vision, because it expresses itself directly in the sonority of the word and in movement. Knowledge or vision can be achieved at another time and in silence. Eurythmy is the meditation that flows directly into the bodily individual, as an encounter of the being of time with the being of space, Therefore, it needs the virtue of spontaneity proper to "rising" thought. Such spontaneity takes back into itself and enchants the power of instincts. It transfers this power to an "area" in which it works for the spirit.

The power of instincts, as a serpentine power, which inevitably emanates from the descent of the movement's virtue, is dominated and transfigured by the person who teaches eurythmy; and thus dominated and transfigured, it operates in the relationship with the disciple. But if the initial commitment of the meditation is lacking in the teacher, the serpentine impetus operates within the movement in place of the light. The movement as an expression of the eurythmic technique becomes estranged from the inspirational element, and operates unconsciously as a vehicle of instinctive forces: in which sensuality is unleashed, subtle and devouring.

The magic of the movement is the immediate expression of universal thought, according to laws realized within the structure of the body: continuously resurfacing in its solemn gait and operating through the limbs in space: resonating in the word, for a further life.

Original willing as the creative word expresses itself in corporeality. The human soul can allow itself to be permeated by the original love living in the mystery of corporeal movement according to the art of eurythmy and surrendering to a higher life, which flows because it is called to conjoin with the corporeal depths where it normally expresses itself through the sleep of consciousness.

But the art of eurythmy is inseparable from a spirit of wisdom and from a lofty morality that does not allow egoity to take possession of the eurythmic technique in order to express itself in brilliant geometrism*. This (geometrism) becomes a destructive magic, destined to paralyze the disciples' conscious life all the way to forms of mental alienation.

---

* geometrism : (philosophy, psychology) A worldview based on geometric thinking or metaphor.
(art) a focus on geometric forms in visual art or the various movements that have engaged it.

10.

Operatio Solis

Mental stillness restores autonomy to the median seat*. It allows the spinal cord's power of spontaneity to express itself before the "I."

In the "primitive" type of human being, the spontaneity of the spinal system is the fundamental force, provided it does not come under the dominion of consciousness. A "primitive" can even be a professor of philosophy at a modern university.

One thing is the "I," another is the consciousness of the "I." This (consciousness) arrests the activity of the "I" at the mental (realm). For this reason, the supra-mental power of the "I" passes unknown in the life of the soul. It flows as the secret life of feeling and of willing.

This gives rise to the head system's opposition to the system of the trunk and limbs: the occult reality of feeling and willing continuously struggles against the deformation of human thinking, which is reflected in the life of instincts and of passions.

In human beings today, it is inevitable that spontaneity be under the sign of longing: that its force be the force of the deviated "I." Whenever we give to this intellectual dignification, a cultural and social situation ensues, which hinders our path.

Only the "primitive" can take the culture of today seriously and unconsciously draw from it the forms necessary for its idolatry.

By virtue of mental silence, the harmonizing force of the median seat—between the seat of thinking and that of willing—is balanced and the breath, which normally is not quiet, quiets down. We breathe because we are restless. We should begin by allowing only the body to breathe.

---

*   Median seat – area of the chest encompassing the heart, the seat of feeling

Mental stillness also gives the spinal cord the autonomy that removes it from the pressure of the ego, restoring the reciprocal independence to feeling and to willing, which is the possibility for them to realize their original harmony within the human being.

The current of the spinal cord, contemplated, is left to connect with the power of life that lies within it, where it can encounter the currents of willing that edify the body, by not corrupting itself in longing.

The autonomy of the spinal cord is the independence of the mental (sphere) from the breath. Those who realize it are free non-rhetorically, and they can go through the world truly knowing the sensory (realm), because they are one in essence with what rules the sensory.

From this autonomy, instincts and passions are recalled as forces in state of rest, which tend to dismiss the egoic form, to manifest their true being.

The breath regards the body, not the "I." What the "I" perceives of the breath, is continuously annihilated by the "I" so that it can arise as its life. The struggle for this annihilation impedes the "I" from breathing directly in its light of life, which is unreflected thinking.

The art is to leave the breath to corporeality, so that it may become to the "I" a perception of its stillness.

***

The autonomy of the spinal cord leads to encountering the "I's" axis of light that normally is interrupted in the head in order to reflect itself as thought.

With reflectivity suspended, what was interrupted only within the area necessary to consciousness, is reconnected. For us as disciples, an incorporeal experience begins that leads us to meet the stellar forces that support the forms and rhythms of creation.

The possibility for us to enter into corporeality ensues. We observe how we are ordinarily outside of it, how we do not really possess the body we believe we are in and through which we have the sense of existing.

Normally, we have the illusion of being in the body. In reality, we have a series of sensations and a correlative image of the body. We believe we are in the body and that the body is ours.

Actually there is nothing that is less ours than the body. If the body were ours, it would never exist, because it would always be destroyed: by thought incapable of life and therefore of truth. The body's secret structure is the adamantine Logos, namely the *phantom* of the Resurrection, which awaits us.

If we have a sufficient grounding in the bodily virtue that we draw out of the sensory—but precisely for this it gives strength to penetrate its inner weft—we can begin to enter into the substantial structure of corporeality, to comprehend how we are not yet truly incarnated in the body.

Human thought does not minimally have the wisdom and knowledge of the thinking that edifies the body. If it had it, the body would not fall ill or die.

The slightest thought with which we are able to take part in corporeal life is enough to demolish and to gradually lead the body to death.

Free of reflected or dialectical thinking, we feel the limitedness of human intelligence and we look at a world of intelligence above it. We begin to partake of the wisdom that lies at the foundation of corporeality. We are worthy to begin feeling ourselves within the power of corporeality, where we gather the uselessness of the ego, whose true force manifests in the suprasensory, freed of sensory tensions.

No obtuse bodily relaxation, yogic or physio-psychological, can do this. On the contrary, it inevitably acts in the opposite way, by binding even more seriously to the animal sensation of the body while also removing the possibility of being aware of it. In the body, only the spirit can be alive and awake.

In ascetic work, worthiness must be achieved. We must justify not being excluded from the body. We are ordinarily excluded from it to the degree that we are bound to the mental picture and to the sensation of the body, and these are mistaken for the body. We are excluded from the knowledge of the forces that support the body and to which we owe the movement of thought. (They are) stellar forces that in the depths of the organs and of the body's architecture refer to other stages of life, expressing themselves in structures of time.

***

Through the autonomy of the spinal cord, we enter into the depths of the corporeal structure and we know that we move in a body woven of time, inserted limitlessly in space; and yet (it is) individual. Beyond all possible human pain, which indicates the profound attachment to the human, we attain this autonomy: which is for the realization of the human.

The rhythm of this movement takes place in true space, in which we enter as into the concrete area of life.

Free in the presence of the "I," the spinal axis incarnates its ancient light. It discovers the sense of its verticality between heaven and earth in the possibility that the members experience, as autonomous spontaneity, the powers of movement that are expressed in earthly space: wherein lies the original wisdom. Autonomous spontaneity operates as the highest form of consciousness.

The spinal axis becomes the vehicle that connects, within corporeality, the heights of the heavens with the depths of the earth, where the body born of the gods is given to the gods in its spontaneous movement.

Inserted as a vertical virtue of the body, it bears within itself, the power of the Divine's descent into earthliness, in that it realizes the virtue of the heights, and can let itself go beyond all space, because the limbs free from physical necessity, or from the neuro-sensory relation, come alive with the same original force and can play in space. Corporeality is launched forward by the spirit as its unstoppable being.

In the spinal cord rendered autonomous by the head system, we have the image of the spontaneity born of freedom and of the corporeal being's participation in the earthly game of forces. The more independence it carries within itself, the more it can participate in this game—the soul being by its structure sacredly turned to the Divine.

Edenic innocence rises again in the experiencer by virtue of this spontaneity, in that it discovers the lower world's original power of expulsion thanks to which cosmic humanity gradually eliminated, in primordial times, the forms that did not respond to the necessity of its earthly incarnation—from which arose the realms of nature. This power must begin rising again as a virtue of the "I," if we want to overcome our lower nature; (if we want) to know what to do with the world of instincts and of passions.

The same power by whose virtue today the metabolic system can expel substances that cannot be used by the forces of life, will rise again as the highest life of the will in spiritual practitioners able to restore, to the spinal system, the ancient light—rekindled in the depths of earthliness thanks to the sacrifice of Golgotha.

In truth the light, restored by the Christ for the redemption of the earth's etheric-physical being, is present in us as a force that operates along the spinal axis. But it is unknown and inaccessible to us, until the day comes that we are able to bring ourselves before the Threshold of the spiritual world, in that area of our being where the profound forces of thought are bound to cerebralism, where we can arrive as we arouse the act of freedom from our own "ego," which can spring only from us—we having died to the vanity of the Earth: so that love might be born of the Earth.

***

The highest spiritual practice leads to feeling the spirit identical to corporeality, inasmuch as the spirit becomes free of the form of mental picturing bound to corporeality.

The stillness actualized in the nervous system makes of it the vehicle of the "I" in the corporeal depths.

The stillness and the void of the nervous system are an identical thing, by means of which the spirit discovers itself as the foundation of corporeality.

Corporeality and the spirit are a single being, from which the being of the "I" in the world begins. The spirit arises unopposed to the body.

The body ceases to be the weight of the soul.

In the body that rests with its very being on earth, the soul feels the earth free itself of gravity.

The soul becomes corporeal, until disappearing into corporeality, as it returns to be the original calm of the spirit.

The body and the spirit actualize the agreement that has the power of reuniting what is separated in the world.

The body is the soul of the "I." Through the body, the spirit gives rise to the soul. The whole operation for the "I" takes place within the soul. What we each truly lack is the soul, so that ordinarily we cannot feel ourselves as a being distinct from our own instinctivity, from our own corporeality. Therefore, we each cannot realize ourselves as an "I." We live conditioned by corporeal consciousness; for this reason, we ignore the corporeal being.

***

Longing, repulsion, pain are the soul's dissonance within the corporeality oppressed by the soul. The soul calms down. The dissonance is known by the soul in its radicalness, because knowledge as a force of love extinguishes the reciprocal oppression of forces. The autonomy of the soul's conscious principle, objectifying the forces, draws agreement from the dissonance.

The body itself does not need to constitute, as a support, opposition to consciousness. The opposition is necessary for a strong awareness only of its own limitations.

Left to rest in its own being, the body becomes the foundation for the earthly being of the spirit—which is the "I" operating in the soul. To be implemented, the "I" must know the power of the darkness to which its life is bound in earthliness. Only as an ego can it enter with its force into the earth. By experiencing the ego, the "I" experiences not only the possibility of freedom, but the only path for realizing it.

Founded on the spirit, the "I" is free of the body. Therefore, it feels the foundation being given in his body. Turned toward the foundation, the deep flows of the soul tend to quiet down; the soul lives as the flow's motionless power in the heart. From the depths of the heart, cosmic thoughts nourish the soul, edifying the foundation.

In the soul, the spirit encounters is own movement as the power of transmuting instincts. The encounter is continuously a transmutation. There is no need to control instincts and emotions, because they arise in the soul, letting themselves be known as forces of the pure principle that knows them.

Only on earth can this principle make the ego the force for the restitution of its celestial status.

The task of the ego is to acquire so much force as to free itself from the necessity of being valid in the physical world, where its worthiness necessarily generates evil and error. The ego becomes animated with such a force in concentration and meditation: (a force) to which it effectively opens, but to whose inner workings it unconsciously and constitutionally opposes.

The ego can develop within itself so much strength so as to be transferred into it in order to die unto itself. It is the ultimate secret of our meditation today. The ego must accumulate so much *internal* power that its excess frees it of the need to be bound to its own form.

Silence is beyond thought, but at its center.

Part of this excess of strength is necessary for the quietness of the ego, that is, for the cessation of its tendency as ego; another (part) must be offered to the spiritual world as the substance in which it manifests for us—the manifestation not yet being able to be directed in us.

Self-consciousness can experience its own forces, but not yet its own essence. It can only begin by knowing its own manifestations and here recognize itself.

***

The "I" finds itself in the physicality of the body, because it can articulate itself in gravity to arrive one day at experiencing the mineral consciousness of the earth.

Without gravity the "I" could not be born, because the "I" would not have the weight of the earth to overcome. Without having weight, it could not actualize its being independent of weight. In fact, there is no weight that does not weigh for the "I" that experiences gravity.

The articulation of the "I" in gravity is the mobility of the body, namely the metaphysical being of the physical body, which consciousness ignores, because it draws itself from gravity, but which consciousness through spiritual practice can experience as an elevating divine force.

The physical body does not exist as a physical entity. It exists so that it can lean on its foundation, which is not perceived. The physical being does not exist but as an image. The error is not to lean on the physical being, which leans on the spirit.

When the "I" feels itself in gravity, it recognizes through corporeality the essential relationship with the world. But such recognition is its essential mental picturing. The "I" can draw itself outside of the body thanks to the activity that it normally needs for mental picturing.

Such activity manages not to identify itself with its reflected forms. It is not the representation, but the very force of representing—namely, the force from whose forms conditioned by the sensory (realm), spiritual practitioners must free themselves, if they want to experience it.

Now the body arises as the conscious power of image. The body and the imagining tend to be one; they are essentially one. This imagining is, in its fabric, as a formative force, identical to the force that edifies the body.

The will can here implement thought, to the extent that thought is free. For the fact of being free, it does not contradict the order of forces by means of which it is the willing that wills the earth and moves corporeality.

Willing can will the earth, because it overcomes gravity. For this reason, the spirit needs the body and needs to endure its weight, until it finds itself identical to the power that edified it.

To move the earth, to express its maximum force, the will, articulated in gravity, must realize its independence from the nervous system.

The emptiness of the cerebral system becomes the vehicle of thinking in the depths of willing.

The emptiness of thought is the possibility for the "I" to actualize its identity with the original force that has formed the body.

We human beings who believe that we live and experience the physical body, are, in essence, barely inserted in the nervous system and even less in the circulatory system. The body's most profound structures are extraneous to us. Only when we begin to live in the "I" independent of the body, do we enter into the depths of such structures. In reality, we enter there each night by virtue of deep sleep. We may deserve to know the mystery of the earth's mineral consciousness.

***

Corporeality and the soul become one. The person who knows how descend into the depths of corporeality lives in the soul according to its transcendence. But to be immersed in corporeality, without falling asleep, we must render the soul independent of the nervous system. Then, the "I" is in the spirit and the spirit is in the world, because it knows its identity with the stellar forces that edify the corporeal being from the earthly realm.

The spirit does not flow if it is limited to the consciousness of itself—if it is limited to being a reflection of the world. Nor will reflectivity ever recognize itself as such, since it can have no other experience outside of reflecting itself.

The art of thinking is to render intense the consummation of reflectivity, which cannot extinguish itself through its own force, emanating from the depths of the skeletal system and the nervous system. The ego is founded upon reflectivity. In that sense, it is the opponent of the spirit, which uses the force of the spirit.

The abstractness of reflected thought and minerality constitute a harmony of forces from which the ego draws life. Such harmony is opposed to the "I," and yet it utilizes for itself the inner forces not endowed with sufficient consciousness.

Concentration and meditation are the art of actualizing the independence of thinking, so that that harmony does not dominate but serves the "I." In fact, hindering entities, which are able to act within the inner human soul, avail themselves, occultly, of such harmony, but not where we each begin to be an "I," a free being.

As the Master of the new times teaches, the forces of representation are drawn from the skeletal and nervous system, namely from the minerality of the human being; whereas the living forces of the will are drawn from the muscular and blood system.

The spirit must be able to articulate itself in the organism of the blood and muscles, to discover its original force paralyzed in the bones and in the nervous system. In that sense, it operates by extinguishing reflected thought and encountering beyond extinguished thought the powers of willing, as forms of a superhuman thinking.

The spirit can perceive the power of life of minerality, of which the mineral being on earth is the deprivation—real and symbolic. It then knows this power of life as the thought of the Hierarchies, in which its "I" lives.

As an organism of forces deprived of spiritual life, the nervous system does not belong to the body. In the body, it functionally represents a process, extraneous and temporary.

The soul cannot unite with supra-sensory corporeality and realize the spirit of corporeality, as long as it depends on the nervous system, as long as it does not recognize this system as the void in which its incorporeal force can surface, which is the spirit.

One must be dead in the nervous system to be alive in the spirit of corporeality and to know that for which the nervous system is devoid of life. The spirit of corporeality is the "I am," the original light rising again within the human being that receives it without corrupting it.

It is necessary to be dead in the nervous system, so that the light of life—of which it was deprived so as be the instrument of consciousness—can be resurrected.

Only its death leads to the experience of the senses, but only the experience of the senses encounters, in the form of death, that lost life of light.

Thinking and perceiving, like human feeling and willing, are possibilities thanks to an encounter of the subtle current drawn from the skeletal-nervous system with that of the blood-muscular system. Here is the sense of earthly life, the one that can respond to metaphysical and cosmological enigmas, now dialectically devoid of meaning.

In this spontaneous encounter, of each day, of each moment, the soul continuously has the opportunity to find the lost life of the spirit.

The spirit discovers its original forces buried in deep corporeality, if it can know the nervous system's path of the void.

***

Normally, our consciousness does not live as the "I" or as the soul. It does not live in the spirit but, rather, in their corporeal-vital reflection.

In the soul's reflection, egoic consciousness compels the soul forces which alter and become destructive to the body, because only in this way can they participate in the life of consciousness.

No one knows what the body is. One knows of its birth and of its death, of its becoming, but it remains in its impenetrable concreteness. *Its birth is not experienced, nor is its death.*

A science of the body does not yet exist. One provides for its animal needs, but one cannot provide for its foundation, because it is unknown. One cannot act upon it. One seeks to combat sickness and one accepts death as inevitable.

Current physiology, though theoretically articulated in an exact analytical system, does not even explain the process of perceiving that renders its investigation legitimate. Regarding the body, it knows only a mechanical relationship of representations.

Medicine, when it is not tradition, proceeds by means of the casual connections of such representative mechanics and the correlative constants; empirics and abstractness dominate its method, involving a dialectics extraneous to the concreteness of the object, which, as a living object, is not in any way experienced. The relation between the human being and the body would be knowable only by the person who noticed the *identity* with the body, and yet glimpsed the path of the *non-identity*, from which one should move.

No investigation is able to penetrate matter and therefore corporeality, because we humans are, within our system of representations, cut off from it. We are unaware of the forces with which we are inserted into corporeality, therefore we do not have them at our disposal. Only in the vivification of thought do we have a way to begin perceiving the forces independent of corporeality. But we must know where the possibility of such vivification begins.

Only by realizing ourselves outside of corporeality can we penetrate its foundation. But it is an operation that we unknowingly begin with the activity of thinking, making the physical structure of the world arise as real, in the cognitive act, by filling the being with matter and not knowing that we do it, thus ignoring its own immaterial reality.

We must make use of the consciousness that arises from corporeality to find ourselves outside of it, namely outside of the sensations and the mental pictures of the body in which we are currently enclosed. Yet, for this reason, we cannot make use of ancient spiritual practices but, rather, of a spiritual practice that enables us to penetrate our present-day mental picturing and the secret meaning of reflectivity.

By overcoming reflectivity, we can enter the incorporeal current of life, which does not require reflection of the body to operate in the human, because it penetrates corporeality from remote regions of the spirit.

By realizing the autonomy of the forces expressed in mental picturing, we know the sacredness of the intellect unreflected and the correlation of this with the autonomy of the spinal cord. We know the non-terrestrial powers that support the body independently of corporeal consciousness. We tend to transfer the forces of the ego into the incorporeal (sphere), there, where this ego has its redemption, because it expresses its true being—extraneous to the sensory sphere.

***

Disciples must not cease to live in the concreteness of the human, even when they intimately begin to experience the light of life within themselves. These are two worlds from which we draw the greatest wisdom, if we know how to keep them separate: because this separation prepares for their synthesis, which is true insofar as it takes place behind the screen of consciousness. We can gather objective matter for the inner experience, in the necessity of common existence. We must regulate ourselves in physical existence according to the laws that this (existence) involves, by accepting its contradiction serenely, because this arouses in us the sense of our human tasks and of the relationship with an order of forces that, at the roots, has resolved the contradiction.

Furthermore, on the outer plane, we must act and move from one sector to another of the human sphere. We must think, speak, work, communicate with others, engage ourselves, struggle. Regarding the inner experience, we need the opposite attitude.

We must cease to become agitated. We must suspend movement; in reality, we have nothing to move.

When our inner experience becomes real, nothing should move from us, because within us *Something* moves that we are not and that does not like to be hindered by other movements. We must only wait in complete stillness, for *Something* that we are not to move in us. Only at our highest will is it possible to wait in silence until the "I am" surfaces in the soul. And it surfaces by means of this intact will. *Something* moves in the soul that transcends it, but it could not move if a higher soul force did not identify with it.

The exhaustion of the mental motion ensues from the possibility of identifying it and mastering it. Disciples know the gateway to the supra-sensory experience as a state of quiet expectation, which demands nothing, because in the sphere of contradictions it does not let prevail that of itself which identifies now with one part, now with another part.

This contradiction in ordinary life is necessary to the ego and involves a struggle for it that never ceases, and yet, it is continuously terminated. It continuously does not exist, because, beyond the field of contrasts, we disciples, thanks to meditation, elicit a subject that is not the ego and brings itself to a state of profound peace and awaited calm of the invisible, where we encounter forces that have overcome human contradiction.

The objective supra-sensory experience is not accessed, unless we pass through such an area of profound calm, where peace with beings subsists unalterable, built in conscious openness to human drama and pain, whose appeasement is the work of the Divine in the human.

***

Free from the mental (sphere), what is had as a sense of the body is dropped. We cease to feel confined to physical existence. Nevertheless, it is as if we finally enter the bodily substance; as if we incarnate in it; or as if we are born in the body. But it is a being born, as well as a disappearing, in it—owing to the temporary disappearance of its limitation.

We enter the body by gradually leaving the supports—vital, sentient, thinking.

To enter the body is to descend into an endless depth, in which we are able to descend, because we bring with us our incorporeal life, the virtue of the heights. It is the extinction of the ego and the intact use of its force.

To descend into the depths of oneself is the art of identifying with the calmness and the infinity that secretly substantiate the body from stellar sources. This identity cannot be an act of the ego, but of the "I."

The body as a finite entity is the illusion of rationalists unaware of the very structure of rationality.

The art is to exit—by way of meditative intensity—the usual form of mental picturing, so as to be free from attachment to the form with which we believe we are in the body.

To leave such a form is to feel it vanish little by little within our own being as it descends into the darkness of the depths, to be absorbed within the foundation.

The descent into the depths of oneself is the highest liberation. Therefore, it is the initial act of comprehending the darkness in which we suffer—the objective act of love. By way of an incorporeal virtue, we enter the transparency of the body, which is its fluctuation of light, in the movement.

The light that becomes movement and that shines in the motion, is the magical will.

Identifying with the body is the soul's disappearance into its original stillness, which is the body rediscovered as an earthly entity—the one from which we were expelled at the dawn of the world.

In essence, to enter the body is to live again as a soul of corporeality, that is, to identify with the forces which, from outside of space, enter earthliness to converge in the corporeal form. We receive the liberating virtue of their movement, beyond the sentiment of the corporeal limit.

The body is the space of the movement.

Such space has no limits: belonging to the stellar world. Corporeality being cosmically one. The celestial human is complete; the earthly human must still become.

In truth, we do not die as a result of bodily destruction, since the body, edified by the Hierarchies, is in itself indestructible. The body dies because the soul corrupts and destroys it, by attaching itself egoically to corporeality and cutting out the spirit, thereby consecrating as real a world and a culture devoid of spirit.

The human body is in itself immortal, because it is founded on the extra-terrestrial forces of the soul and of the spirit. Spiritual practitioners operate by means of the will to restore the foundation to earthly human beings. This undertaking is called *Operatio Solis* by disciples of the Rose Cross.

The body's immortality is the restoration toward which the spirit proceeds from life to life experiencing death, namely the death that during our existence is perpetuated in abstract thought and in the breath, in the feeling and in the willing of the ego—in dialectics.

***

The breath only minimally enters into the preparation of Operatio Solis. As physical breath, it is essentially extraneous to it.

The extraneousness is the measure of the breath's cooperation, which is to say, of the realization of its stillness.

The intervention of the breath is always an unconscious oppositional motion, insofar as it excludes the spirit. It is to draw life from a corporeality that the soul separates from the spirit and therefore destroys, while the task of the soul is to open up to the spirit to draw from it the relationship with corporeality. The intervention of the breath is to ask nature for a vitality that has been deprived of spiritual nourishment. It is a form of fear that goes unnoticed—fear that feeling must free itself from the egoic oppressions. In these oppressions, feeling is yearningly rooted.

We must train ourselves not to be afraid of sinking into ourselves. We must strive for the courage of not needing support, of leaving the support on which we unknowingly still support ourselves.

We always support ourselves. But, suddenly, we discover that this support is illusory, that wanting to support ourselves is to renounce supporting ourselves. It is to renounce being truly alive.

There is no need to lean on anything, if the "I" begins to be.

The one who leans, cannot hold on.

The one who wants to hold on, has not understood.

***

Liberation from the support knows no contradiction. What follows from this liberation is unexpected, because it springs from the original being, unable to be conditioned by the world already made, which it made and always makes anew.

The free emergence is the spontaneity restored in its purity.

Contradiction, doubt, the call to an opposite and different movement, regard the intellect, not the inner choice, which unforeseeable and secure goes from essence to essence. What is freely chosen is right, being before the possibility of infinite variation; containing them all is thought capable of being conscious in its fullness by means of single determination.

In the supra-sensory (realm), proceeding is the progressive encounter with reality, without the intervention of the intellect, without the soul's reaction. The soul's presence is its silent dedication and its conscious annihilation, in which the true being manifests.

The soul's intervention is a possibility *a posteriori*. Occurring during supra-sensory experience, it is the impediment. It means that we are still incapable of truly leaving the support. Any movement of the soul, at this point, must not come from the soul but, rather, from its identification with that which transcends it. But in that case it should not be experienced, if the "I" truly contemplates the world of forces: just as one who walks observing a landscape is not attracted by the movement of the legs.

We must not utilize the liberation from the support, nor enjoy it, nor take advantage of it, nor translate it into dialectics, nor feel it as something that is possessed, because it is not true; (we must) not feel it as something to be valued within human being, because then it is already lost, and we are unaware of having already lost it. The greatest spiritualistic presumptions arise from having unknowingly lost it.

Liberation from the support is the relation with ourselves and with the world removed from the ego. It is a relation that normally belongs to the ego, which exists only on the basis of the relation's breakdown. The ego lives by its own attachment to the world—codified, made ethical, and religiously sublimated.

The relation removed is the death of the ego. The death of the ego is its resurgence in the supra-sensory.

But it is necessary for the ego to exist, so that it can die.

***

There is no human use of liberation, because liberation itself, by being there, orients the human being. The translation of freedom in human terms is the capacity of self-determination, so that we can truly love our neighbor, by subordinating ourselves to what is recognized as necessary for the elevation of the other.

To love our neighbor as ourselves, when real, is the human equivalent of the highest initiatic achievement.

The proof of this is the possibility of fully accepting the sphere of necessity, that is to say, the acceptance—according to the spirit of the sense world, regardless of the form posed by necessity—of pain, of death, of sickness, of poverty, of dishonor. All this, if it is imposed, can be accepted as that which gives the measure of the inner presence in the experience, of the noetic overcoming of legitimate notions regarding the mystery of *karma* and of freedom, of independence from the earth's illusory values, upon which the ego builds its security.

Without "ego" the spirit could not act upon the earth. The spirit can operate in the ego, until it lives off its death.

Necessity is only the sensory world. To speak of inner necessity has no meaning. The ego is the obscurity necessary for the spirit's penetration into the sensory (realm). Outside the sensory, it is the principle of the force. But it is the force that can be elaborated only in the sense world.

To enter corporeality means to encounter the sacred powers of the human being: real as supra-sensory.

Therefore, the sacrifice of the "ancient being" is the path. The ancient being tends, from the sub-conscious, to restore in a mysterious or cadaverous order, the forms of its elapsed earthly domain and it can succeed in this by means of the ego, whose profound impulse is not to escape its own limitation, and even tell fables of the escape itself, by means of ascetic doctrines and ritualistic science, which once had the positive function for the entity that in them is extinguished and wants to live of its dead being. For them alone matter is true, which they call illusory, so that it remains what it appears to be.

Those revived sacred sciences amount to the most refined egoism for modern human beings. What does not cost overcoming oneself is easy. Therefore it is immediately accepted on the basis of persuasive demonstrations: persuasive because, however, despite the esoteric assumption, they appeal to the brilliant resources of modern dialectics—philology, analysis of symbol and of myth, pure logical thought. What does not require true work on oneself, nor a willful tragic destruction of the ego, is quickly accepted by simple spiritual researchers, because it involves contents that they already contain within themselves. No new movement, unexpected and uncomfortable. The ego is a very astute conservator, feigning everything that can keep its dominion unaltered.

The ego lives buried in the ancient being: ruled by this (being) through the imaginative element enslaved to the obtuse sensory experience of modern humans. In reality, the operators of the "ancient being" are the current Obstructers of the human being.

The death of the ego is possible, if such an imaginative element is volitionally annihilated. Attachment to the body is not really such, because it ignores the body. It is in fact the attachment to sensation and to the sensory image of the body. All the idols of life today arise from such an attachment that values only what is corporeal and useable corporeally.

That imaginative element, in its illusoriness, has magical power, by means of which humans are enslaved by the Obstructers to new idols, which do not appear as idols because they shine with modernity.

We must enter into this magic without being caught, by virtue of true magic.

***

Sinking into corporeality begins to be true when it radically ceases to involve the breath: by implementing independence from it.

Identity with the body is the true independence from the body, insofar as it realizes within the soul the radicalness of the spirit—namely, its immanent virtue, whose measure is the extraneousness of the breath.

No impediment can then be found. One knows that there is no other obstacle to such sinking, except the residual series of mental figurations or of doubts, or of the illusory contrasts, possible in an area that is now immersed in its righteous silence.

Nothing can impede the actualization of what already exists. In essence, there is only to realize the spirit of what is organically completed, because each of us is such a spirit, but ordinarily we feel it to be identical to the body, of which we have only the image. The body is already made. It is the irreversible past.

The body is all the past.

It is not a question of doing anything new, but of not impeding the spirit's perception of itself. This is truly the "new." The spirit does not know it yet. The possibility of reversibility, which begins within thinking, is the possibility of a vision that in the spirit is already completed. There is, first, no philosophy or logic that can grasp the meaning of the world.

To descend into the depths of oneself is to connect with the forces that have built the body and that dominate matter, beyond the birth and death of the body. Death is necessary to us, as a metaphysical measure of the loss of such forces in the sensory experience.

***

The reality that can be known through the senses is supra-sensory, but we believe it to be sensory because we fail to notice how it comes into being in the sensory act. It is known by means of the nervous system, but it has no relationship with it.

Each cognitive act actually occurs, even for brief moments, outside of the nervous system. This extraneousness of the cognitive act from the nervous system is the supra-sensibility continuously realized, unconsciously, in the interests of consciousness, which as *egoic consciousness,* is implemented by destroying the supra-sensory forces that in the body govern physicality and, yet, render it knowable. It is the destruction that renders death inevitable, since it is not known nor its process imagined.

The state of absolute simplicity consequent to sinking into corporeality, leads to the recognition of that supra-sensory motion, ordinarily implemented in the cognitive act, but ignored, which is valid (in its being known, as a death of the ego to the life of the senses) for its supra-sensory birth. The activating of the ego outside of sensory values is its true freedom, its future destiny—the rebirth from its dying.

The force that is developed in egoism must not be ignored nor opposed. Transferred into the supra-sensory, it loses the destructive character, which solely depends on its being exclusively founded on the values of the senses. It then becomes the central virtue of human evolution.

Simplicity is attained, to the extent that the subjective projection of the world is eliminated, due to the wrong use of sensory perception and therefore to the prevalence of the ego in the sensory world. The subject identifies with the essence of entities, if the ego realizes death in the world of the senses: not to dissolve itself, but to experience its own individuating impulse outside of such a world, which is the principle of the sensory experience, of which we are still incapable.

To sink into corporeality is to have overcome the head system, to have relived, as an experience of death, the process for which consciousness arises by means of the cerebral organ.

***

In essence, each of us, insofar as we immediately think, knows how to produce a thought. The art is to know how to reproduce, by virtue of the will, the arising of thought. This arising can be perceived. This perceiving is to transfer the force of the ego, there, where it ceases to be an impulse of death; there, where it can only be the virtue of life. At this point, the ultimate meaning of the "path of thinking" becomes clear.

The error of the ego is its steadfastness toward the sensory world, but it is the first unavoidable way of expressing its own entity. In reality, the ego must discover the absurdity of willing something in the sensory world. Only the "I" can will in the sensory (world), because it has its supra-sensory counterpart. The ego is the force of the "I" that binds itself to the sensory for the long work of structuring earthly brotherhood.

At a given moment, the tenacity of the ego is transferred to the supra-sensory world, where its centripetal force becomes valuable as the capacity of resoluteness against the constraints and pitfalls of the Obstructers.

The ego is inevitably the bearer of the error, of the lie and of evil, for the fact that it exists and wills solely in relation to the sensory world. But it must develop an attachment to the sensory, as a force, so that this force can one day be used by the spiritual principle, outside of the sensory. Loving one's neighbor as oneself, total disinterest, and the capacity of consecration to what illuminates and frees us can no longer be mystical attainments. They can now arise solely from the intellectual transformation of a force that is formed in the sensory darkness.

The capacity for the noetic transposition and therefore the redemption of such a force is the art of meditation. The ego that ceases to will in the sensory, and yet wills beyond, is the presence of the higher "I" in the human being, and the possibility for us to effortlessly realize the impulse given by Christ.

The art is to know where and how to place a force that already exists and that nevertheless we still do not know how to objectively experience. Whoever of us is able to realize as our act what we normally realize according to spontaneity, enters into the secret of reality—into thinking, into feeling and into willing.

Spontaneity ceases to be nature. It returns to being spirit. The spirit operates as spontaneity.

The sinking into oneself is the path of absolute simplicity.

The ego is not to be eliminated, but known. There is no point in wanting to get rid of the ego, without knowing what it is, without it revealing its secret, the sense of its radical being at the center of earthly experience.

Each human being, thanks to the ego, places him or herself at the center of the world. The task is for such a center to be *really* achieved, because it is then the starting point for fraternity.

***

We call it sinking into oneself, entering into the secret corporeality, resting in profound stillness, but it is what can be comprehended only by someone who has known the death of thought and the ego as a force of death.

It is the annihilation of oneself from which alone the intuition of the profound identity with the other can spring, as a reason for fraternity. True knowledge is fraternity. Actually, it is its only foundation.

This sinking into the body is to leave the body and to simultaneously be in the intimacy of its life. It is to be the soul of the body, according to the spirit, not the body.

The more we sink into it, the more we are capable of enduring—without being overwhelmed—the powers from which the ego is drawn from the body. Better than enduring them, is identifying with the stillness in which it is actually founded. One can identify with this stillness, insofar as the ego ceases to draw the unconscious nourishment from instincts. These (instincts), by not encountering their constrictor, free themselves from the basal automatism and tend to elevate themselves, by harmonizing in an impulse, where the imprint of the ego is sublimated as the will of oneself in another (person)—compassion. It is the relation rediscovered with entities that bear the weight of corporeality and that suffer the illusion of bearing such weight.

Being in the depths of the physical being, one can say of the body: it is this.

The essential stillness from which the inexhaustible movement arises is achieved. The movement that is not exhausted is the love that creates.

Touched is the quiet secret of minerality from which the swirling powers of the earth emanate, namely the guardians of an area, invisible and, nonetheless, forthcoming, or rather, intimate to the human being: of a life of light far from visible earthliness and, yet, lying within its secret fabric, as a germinal virtue of the planet's new existence, whose essence urges in us as the "I am"—the one that for now we are capable of being only in the obtuse form of the ego.

Essential stillness is reached when we are able to encounter, congealed in minerality, the thought of the world—that thinks the corporeality. Such thought is rekindled of its original light.

Eden is discovered; the "I am" is restored. But we must connect life with it, the urge of human suffering, thought.

To sink into oneself is to enter into the divine rest that sustains the earth; into the thinking where the 'already-thought' is removed from that irreversibility, which is the evil of the world, namely the necessity of the ego and yet of bodily decay and dying.

***

To descend into the depths of oneself is the path of dedication and of courage.

We become excluded from this path, if we do not know how much we are taken by worldly values, even by those that may be of ethical and cultural necessity.

This path is precluded to those who are taken by their own dialectics, by personal sentiments, by personal spiritual problems, which are not problems of the spirit. It is precluded to those who fail to notice that they are putting the calls of the world before the ultimate commitment of meditation, which alone leads to the comprehension of beings and to the possibility of operating according to their real demand.

It is meditation known discursively and, therefore, actually never truly practiced, because it is always mistaken as a means to restore the peace of consciousness and the rhythm of the physical body.

We must have the courage to see our own vanity before the supra-sensory demand, which cannot be met by a world of cultural, metaphysical, mystical wishful thinking. Thus we presume to be the helpers sought by humanity in danger, whereas we are not even capable of helping ourselves, because we do not know where our evil, our weakness is rooted. We do not want to search where our own force arises. We are afraid of being free, responsible for ourselves, and of ceasing to accuse our neighbor for our own sins. In fact, there exists no evil for which those who endure it are not responsible.

Courage is to recognize the innocence of who appears guilty, of who seems to harm us, or hurt us, so as to not react toward them with aversion but, rather, with knowledge—which is not sentimentalism or weakness, but, rather, the logical equivalence of the most lucid initiatic noesis. Courage is to recognize such equivalence, in order to love our neighbor as ourselves, especially there, where humanly we would have reason for the just revenge, or for a valid accusation. What accuses, criticizes, judges and condemns is never the "I," but the ego, namely the ego with its own morals, its own law, its own tradition, its own spirituality, its own dignity. And as long as the ego conditions the movements of the soul, it cannot be free.

Courage is to see our own incapacity of charity, of tolerance, of spiritualistic rhetoric, absence of spontaneity, vanity, presumption and evil, which teem again with authoritarianism and that irresistibly tend to identify themselves with the forces of the soul, just awakened by meditation.

The way of the spirit, certainly, is open to everyone. Each of us advances along our own path, which leads to the "way," but it is not the "way." The direction is indeed unknown, because, even if it has been given, it is not sufficient—as has been shown—to learn it from texts or oral transmissions. Only courage illuminates the direction.

Ritual action is required of very few, to whom is offered as a trial or as help, the possibility of betraying. But, it belongs to the very few or to rare individuals; it belongs to more; this way demands the righteousness that comes from courage—the courage to love our neighbors according to the "I am", because only from the "I am" can a relationship with the world arise that is not illusory. The sign of the presence of the "I am" is the realization of love for the other in the sphere of the will, thanks to the perception of the sacred and eternal element present in each creature. This is therefore not like a mystical exaltation but, rather, like a logical crowning of the spiritual practice of thinking, according to its essential light.

The world cannot be transformed by intellectuals, by politicians, or by scientists. These are simply the executors of what can be prepared as a radiant moral force by initiates, capable of connecting themselves with the profound Being of the destiny of peoples, the Spirit of the time, or the "Ancient of Days."

In truth, one must know what one is talking about; *not talk about what one does not know.*

Today, the impulse to betray is inevitable for everyone; it is the test for everyone, being the position of uncontrolled abstract thought and continuously led to mistake the discursive corpse of truth for the being of truth. Betrayal is the expositive vanity, under whose esoteric fiction instincts regurgitate in the state of renewed and codified imperiousness.

The danger of losing righteousness today looms especially over those who presume to teach, to hold flowery speeches, enjoying the ecstatic attention of others to whom they transmit teachings, which indeed cannot pass through oratory or mysteriosophical excitation.

By cultivating such vanity, we are excluded from the "way." The texts of wisdom, even the most confidential, the norms of "group reunions" and secret rituals may be known; we may have received, orally, the decisive techniques of inner development. All this remains unheeded. Instead, it becomes food for individualistic presumption, if it does not move from the spirit from which it originates, if it cannot immediately manifest as impersonality, dedication to the other being—if it cannot be realized as the capacity to love any human creature as oneself.

In truth, we transmit to others only what we have been able make of our own radical individualism. The consciousness soul, in its immediacy, presents itself as evil equipped with thinking security, but incapable of being recognized as evil.

In order to be real, the birth of the consciousness soul demands that the motion of pure thinking be identical to the motion of love, which means the emergence of the "I am" within the soul.

***

The art of ancient ascetics was to arrive at self-forgetfulness to the point of dying before the sensory world. In the quiet depths, they let the fog of instincts and of passions vanish. They lost the sense of the earthly. Detachment, elusiveness, apathy, ataraxia were forms of their dying to the sensory (realm).

It was an art of a human type, whose system of nerves bore the last resonances of the original light. It was not yet lifeless and therefore dominated by the physicality of the world, having still, albeit as a memory, some inner life. Thus, for this human type abstract thought was not yet possible nor was sensory perception devoid of a supra-sensory content.

A system of nerves that had not isolated human beings, but had continued to connect them with the supra-sensory, would not have been able to be the mediator of the concrete, sensory and individual experience—the one necessary for the experimentation of a completely earthly ego, without which the spirit cannot extract the forces that only from earthliness can reach them.

An estrangement from sensory life and a mystical order that avoids worldly experience, as well as religiosity incapable of justifying metaphysically the science of nature and of penetrating the mystery of sensory life, a mystery hermetically forbidden—as we have seen—even to the abstract science of the physical world, are a more subtle form of egoism that can still impede our path.

Ancient ascetics could easily estrange themselves from the contingency of the outer world, because the same nervous system that provided them the experience of the senses and gave them its knowledge of the depths, connected them to the spiritual world. For them it was enough to close the door to the senses, in order to penetrate into the supra-sensory. Meanwhile, we modern human beings, by means of the nervous system, can have no other experience except that of the senses and of the thinking tied to them.

By isolating themselves from the sensory, ancient ascetics could attain, through the nervous system, a profound stillness similar to death. Their art was to know the secret for attaining such a symbolic death, therein being helped by gods for which the occasion of their conscious freedom did not arise.

We as spiritual practitioners of the present time do not need this death, because it is already carried out in the nervous system and in the life of the ego. The importance of the ego is to bear into its life the power of its death. Without this power, there is for us no possibility of restoring light and immortality.

Today, we, as spiritual practitioners, do not need to kill the ego. We only need to know ourselves, so as to encounter the death of the ego, already completed, namely the death on which the activity of consciousness is based and what, according to it, we consider alive.

Our path cannot be the one that closes the doors of the senses, because our nervous system is no longer the vehicle of supra-sensory experience, but only of the experience of the senses and of the correlative thinking, by means of which, instead, we can consciously discover the supra-sensory. The experience of the senses—as we have seen—must be carried out by the spirit, which realizes through it the transcendence of what, as sensory appearance, binds it to earthliness.

Death, or dis-animation, of the nervous system, is the possibility for us, as thinking human beings, to experience the void, the darkness, nothingness, already realized. We can encounter them in ourselves, within the physical support of consciousness. As we have shown in the preceding pages, what presents itself as a barrier to the spiritual world is the doorway to it. It is a matter of opening our eyes, of seeing what is indeed present in perceiving, in everyday thinking, in pain and in corporeal destruction. What appears to be reality is none other than the death of a world that is continuously alive, as the imperceptible movement of perceiving and of thinking.

The spiritual practitioner of today must grasp thinking and know its state of death, so as to penetrate it and arrive, there, where this death is tangible—in the structure of the ego, which sensory life draws from the highest forces that have fallen into earthliness.

Death perceived becomes life, by virtue of a resurrection secretly founded on the Logos, in the substance of the Earth, that can be experienced today by the free human being.

Along these lines, the death of abstract thought, realized, is the death of egoism, knowable as the path of sacred magic, whose function is to give rise—from the profound annihilation—to new forces at the roots of the soul of a minimal core of human beings, if the moral catastrophe taking place is to avoid overwhelming civilization.

Spiritual practitioners can experience such death, by perceiving within it the disappearance of dialectical whims and earthly tensions. We must experience a death, in which we normally live without knowing the secret for which we can nevertheless live in it.

The brain that can know its own death, opens within the human being, the threshold to the healing of the evil of death. It begins to draw life from something other than nature. In knowing its foundation as silence, it realizes the non-being of its earthliness, which was necessary for the birth of thought and the immediate death of this thought, of which we still live, in anticipation of being worthy that the mystery of the Resurrection open up to us.

The brain, led to volitionally and sacrificially realize the death of which it is structured, fundamentally returns to being one with the original thinking, woven of light that until now it has reflected, in order to shine one day of the sound of this ancient light.

This is the secret, veiled and unveiled, in the present book.